SHADOWS ON MY SHIFT

Real Life Stories of a Psychic EMT

Sherri Lee Devereau

SHADOWS ON MY SHIFT: REAL LIFE STORIES
OF A PSYCHIC EMT Copyright ©2006 by Sherri Lee Devereau.
All rights reserved. Printed in the United States of America. No
part of this book may be used or reproduced in any manner
whatsoever without the written permission of the publisher,
except in the case of brief quotations. For information, address
New River Press, 645 Fairmount Street, Woonsocket, R.I. 02895,
(800) 244-1257, books@newriverpress.com

New River Press Web site is: www.newriverpress.com

Cover by Frank Rivera

FIRST EDITION

ISBN: 1-891724-08-8
ISBN 13: 978-1-891724-08-4

To my family, whom I love and cherish
with my whole heart and soul.

Contents

Introduction 5
1. In the Thick of Things 7
2. Holidays and Halos 20
3. Getting Started 27
4. China 38
5. Into Practice 46
6. Convincing the Dead 50
7. Energies 58
8. Night Shift 65
9. Learning Boundaries 71
10. Angels and Working Girls 79
11. The Plot Thickens 87
12. The Call I Recall 99
Final Thoughts 108
Glossary 112
Acknowledgments 116

Introduction

This book is a series of stories dealing with my experiences on the Phoenix Fire Department Crisis Response vans. Obviously, situations, names, locations and dates have been changed to protect the privacy of the public.

While working with the Fire Department, please understand that I am first and foremost an emergency medical technician (EMT), and in a very far second, I am an intuitive who receives messages from those who are about to cross over.

On almost every emergency call I go on, combining these two responsibilities presents an overwhelming dilemma. I do not wish to add more suffering to someone who is already traumatized to their very core, but if I unexpectedly blurted out personal messages from the "other side," it could push them right over the edge.

My professional capacity was not to serve as their "medium," but rather to assist them with immediate, front-line healing. I had to remember that at all times.

This book is about how I dealt with those messages and the inventive ways I was forced to devise in order to deliver them to loved ones who were grieving, all this while under the radar of the unsuspecting, non-believing, "normal" world.

Therein lies the true joy of my existence

-Sherri Lee Devereau, 2006

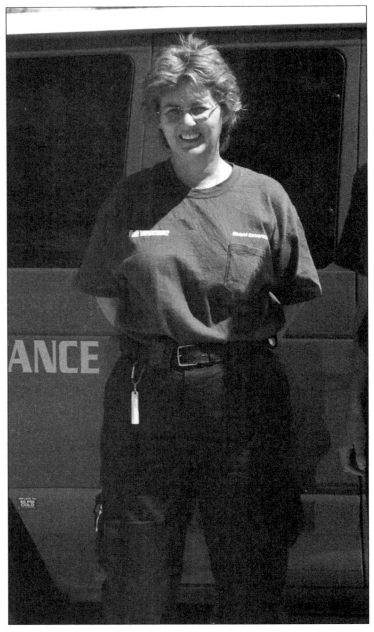

The author on Crisis Response Team duty in Phoenix, Arizona.

1
In the Thick of Things

It's two in the morning, and I'm standing in the middle of a freeway. Sirens are blaring. Red and blue lights are flashing, and reflecting back to blind me. A helicopter overhead shines its spotlight on a scene of twisted metal. The mayhem seems far too surreal at this hour. I hear the fire captain barking commands to firefighters as they feverishly cut, rip and tear at a car so they can reach the driver. Medics stand by with lifesaving equipment. Past scenarios replay in their minds as they anxiously wait to take their turn in this all-or-nothing race against time.

I feel a cool, energy-filled breeze swoosh up my back and swirl around me on this breezeless summer night in Phoenix, Arizona. I know then, in that moment, that they are going to be too late to save this person.

As I stand in the middle of the freeway, in the middle of the night, in the middle of chaos, calmness slowly engulfs me. This feeling is followed immediately by confusion and fear. I sense another presence approaching. It's the deceased driver of the mangled car that's scattered across the freeway.

I try to communicate with the driver, whom I now feel or sense very near me, by opening and heightening my sense of awareness. I tune in to him. As I make that psychic connection, I tell him he has a choice. He can either get back into his body, or go toward the light and love that will soon beckon to him. Those are his only choices as I know them to be.

I feel his confusion and fear: He's not sure what's happening to him, and his searching, fearful energy keeps coming back toward me. I explain to him that he died in a car accident. His energy stills for a moment, and I feel his acceptance of what I've told him. He lets me know he feels a pull to go toward the light because he hears his father, who died the previous year, calling to him. He wants me to tell his mother he was wearing his seatbelt and that he loves her. I make a mental note of his request, and tell him I'll make sure his mother knows.

At this point, I haven't been asked to deliver the death notification, but maybe the driver knows something I don't. I turn to check on my partner, making eye contact. When I turn back, I no longer feel the driver's presence.

As the accident is cleared, a police officer approaches to ask if we'll help him deliver the death notification. This will be his first experience, and he's heard that we're real "pros" at this kind of thing. My partner and I agree, and we make our way to our Fire Department van. We inform the Alarm Dispatch Room that we're moving to another location to deliver a death notification.

I can hear it in their voices -- they don't envy me right now. Although I've done hundreds of these calls over the years, it never gets easier.

The sun breaks free of the horizon, heating the early morning air as it conquers the sky. We approach the front door of an older, ranch-style home. We let the officer take the lead. I stand behind him, with my partner behind me, as the officer knocks on the door. A woman answers, still in her bathrobe. She's not prepared for the three of us standing before her so early in the morning. She stands voiceless for a moment, not knowing if she wants to greet us or shut the door on us.

I nudge the officer from behind, and he introduces us. I ask if we can come inside to talk with her. It takes a moment for the woman to realize that this isn't a social visit. She pales a bit, and her hand shakes as she opens the door to invite us into her lovely home. The first thing I notice is the large number of family pictures on the walls. We all take seats in the living room, and the police officer begins to ask the woman a few questions to make sure we're in the right place.

Unfortunately, for her, we are.

As the officer continues with his questioning, I look around. I see a familiar face hanging on the wall, and as I make that mental connection, I again feel that cool burst of air, mixed with energy. I double check to make sure the air conditioning hasn't kicked in. It hasn't. I can safely assume the young driver is here with us, watching, sending his love to his mother.

The officer clears his throat and starts to say why we're here, but he stops and looks at me, his eyes pleading for me to step in. I feel the cool flow of energy swirl around me even more as I prepare to speak.

"My name is Sherri. I'm with the Phoenix Fire Department. I'm sorry to inform you that your son has died."

I tell this grieving mother that her son was killed in a car accident that wasn't his fault. I reassure her, when she asks, that he had been wearing his seatbelt at the time of the crash. She shares with me that they had a secret between them. She had told him that wearing a seatbelt was like being hugged by your mom and being protected by angels, all at the same time. He'd promised he would always wear his seatbelt, and send the love back to her when she wore hers. I remind her that each time she buckles her seatbelt, she'll get that hug from her son, who will now be her personal angel.

Most of these visits begin the same way: my name, the organization I'm with, and then the bad news. I'm a volunteer on the Crisis Response (CR) vans with the Phoenix Fire Department. The CR van has teams of people specially trained by the Fire Department to handle unique, and sometimes tragic, calls. CR teams consist of two members per twelve-hour shift, an emergency medical technician (EMT) and a behavior health specialist (BHS).

The EMT usually drives the van and is charged with getting the team to the call safely. He or she also is responsible for the physical health of the people being assisted. EMTs must be state certified and must keep their certifications up to date.

BHSs are the "touchy-feely" ones of the group. Many are college students working on their counseling or social-work degrees. Working with Fire Departments allows them to accumulate the one-on-one counseling hours necessary to graduate. They're responsible for the mental and emotional well being of the people they're assisting. A BHS team member also can partner with another BHS to qualify as a CR team.

CR teams of either combination are dispatched by Alarm room personnel. The Alarm room is where 9-1-1 calls are answered and dispatched to the police and Fire Departments. Teams are sent into all sorts of situations, including "codes" (when someone dies), shootings, stabbings, drownings, domestic-violence calls, giving death notifications, assisting people with coping problems, as well as any other kind of call that combines trauma with drama.

Our job as a crisis response team is to assist the families or individuals with the issues they face at that moment. Calls can last anywhere from a few minutes to several hours, depending on the need. Each call is unique.

I'm again driving the never-ending freeways of Phoenix. Early, pre-Christmas dawn slowly stretches into the sky, casting a warm, friendly glow on the windshields of passing cars. I glance down at the map to make sure I remember the right freeway exit. I'm going to a new station today, and I'm a bit nervous. Making a good first impression is important to me.

I finally find the fire station, pull up to the long metal security gate, and punch in the security code. The gates magically open.

"So far, so good," I think to myself. I park on the far side of the station and hope I didn't take someone's favorite spot. I gather my gear from the trunk of my car (a jacket, hat, sunscreen, snacks, and the Phoenix Crisis Care Handbook), and walk toward the station's three big, open bay doors. I see my partner waiting. What a relief! It's my friend Andrea.

We were in training class together many years ago. This is going to be a great shift because we can catch up on each other's lives if we don't get too busy. We hug each other, laugh and head toward the van to begin our mandatory, pre-shift supply check-off procedure. When we're almost done, we decide to make our van available for calls. We push the "Available on Radio" (AOR) as we continue to chitchat and check out the vehicle.

Within minutes, the fire station "tones" go off, calling us into service. Tones are very loud noises that fill the bay (where fire engines are parked and ready to go) and our quarters with specific warning notes, hence the name. They're accompanied by blinding lights, followed by the dispatcher's voice saying what type of call it is and where.

It's 2 a.m. I grab the radio's microphone, hanging on the bay wall, and let the alarm room know we heard and acknowledge the call. It's a code, which means someone has ceased breathing and has no pulse. In every sense of the word, he or she is dead. Paramedics are called out to try and get a pulse back and to restore breathing.

This doesn't always work. Sometimes the person has been "down" without proper amounts of oxygen for too long to even attempt a revival. Regardless, the CR team is called out to assist family members in dealing with this dramatic event.

We try to chase Bobcat, the station's adopted kitten, out of our van. He's decided to go along and has squeezed his way into the most inaccessible part of the vehicle. He's a strange mix of cat breeds, looking to be part Manx because of his funky, stubby tail. I can only guess that's why the firefighters dubbed him "Bobcat."

Bob finally streaks out of the van, and we make a mad dash

to the bathroom. First rule on the van is to always "go" whenever you can. You never know when or how long it'll be before you get another chance!

Andrea and I jump into the van and start the checklist. I press a button on our computer that lets the dispatchers know that we're on our way. Andrea gets the mapping system up on the computer screen, ready to lead us to our destination. With a push of a button, the big bay doors swing open, and we're off.

A code is never the best run to make, especially near major holidays. Someone has passed, and we have to break the news to their loved ones. Crisis Response Team members are trained to assist people through the first few hours of grieving by helping them notify other family or friends, select a funeral home, and by offering general information about what happens next. Holidays are supposed to be a time of celebration, not mourning.

As an intuitive, medium and psychic, as well as an EMT, codes take on a different dimension for me than for the others. Everyone in this job sees dead people on shift, but I also hear them, making my involvement far more interesting, as well as more complicated. I must remain professional, so I often can't pass along messages from the deceased right away, forcing me to find other ways to deliver that final communication.

As Andrea and I pull up to the YMCA, we see a fire truck and a rescue (ambulance) unit working on someone lying on the ground next to the building. Andrea pushes a button on the computer to let dispatch know we're now on-scene.

As we get out of the van, we don latex gloves and approach the crowd surrounding the patient, an older gentleman. Firefighters are working feverishly to save him. We step aside as they rush past us to load him into the rescue unit. With lights and sirens blaring, they're off to the closest available hospital emergency room. Andrea and I jump into our van and give chase. We can't use lights and sirens, and we're required to obey the speed limits, so it takes us longer to reach the hospital.

Once there, it takes us awhile to convince the over-zealous front desk personnel to buzz us through the emergency-room (ER) double doors. The ER is filled with no less than seven people working hard to save the unidentified man's life. This is a very small hospital and, at first glance, grossly understaffed. The security guard pulls double duty. His secondary assignment is to contact other wards in the hospital to locate the right vials of medicine to fill the doctors' orders. Once he finds the ward that has the medicine, he runs to that floor, gets the medicine, and runs back down to the ER. We watch him do this several times over the next thirty minutes.

We decide to walk over to make small talk with a sheriff's officer as she sits next to a handcuffed prisoner who's also a patient. We ask the officer what his story is. She tells us he has a major warrant for failure to pay child support over the last few years. He had started the day drinking in a bar, got into an argument, started a fight, and ended up in Sheriff Joe Arpaio's famous tent-city jail. Once this man knew he was going to jail, he faked chest pains and was rushed to the hospital. There he lay on a gurney, pretending, when just a few feet away a man fought for his life.

Sadness overcomes me for this handcuffed man, for his children, and for the life he'll never have with them. But I know by the cool feeling of energy flowing around me that these aren't my thoughts but those of the man from the YMCA.

Rapid flashes of pictures and feelings race through my mind: his regrets, losses, sadness, and disappointment in himself for how he has lived his life. It begins to overwhelm me. He wants me to tell this handcuffed man all that he'll be missing, and what's at stake. But I can't do that. I tell the YMCA man that it's not my job today. His energy weakens and pulls away, which can only mean one thing – the medical team is getting some type of heartbeat back.

I head over to see what's happening. I stand there transfixed, watching as the medical team uses four different drugs to revive the YMCA man. The only intravenous (IV) line they can get on this man is in the groin area because he has no blood pressure. This patient didn't drink or do drugs. He held a steady job, and people we later talked with spoke of him as a great man. I watch as two members of the ER's support team reach exhaustion after repeated rounds of cardio pulmonary resuscitation (CPR).

The doctor looks up and spots me standing there. Our eyes meet and lock. I know then that this is going to be bad news for me. He motions for me to step in and continue with the chest compressions. I look behind me. Seeing no one, I look at him again. He's much more insistent and animated this time as he motions me forward, pointing to an open spot next to him.

I take a deep breath and step into the curtained-off area. All my senses are at peak attention. I feel the cool breeze of energy alerting me to the YMCA man's presence now filling the room, the very thing I was dreading. This man's soul is out of his body, and he knows I can communicate with him. As I step up onto the small stool next to the gurney, I look down onto his blue-tinged face and know we won't get a "save" on this one, but I just had to try.

The EMT in me takes over, and I want that save as much as everyone in that room does. I position myself and wait for the doctor's nod.

I begin compressions and sense that the deceased wants to be left alone. He wants all of us to stop trying to bring him back. He lets me know he's tired and wants to move on. He also communicates that he no longer has any pain in his body for the first time in years, and that he feels like a kid again. He wants me to stop, to let him go. I continue to count with each compression and try to tune him out, but it's not working. I continue doing my part of the CPR as the doctor barks orders for more drugs.

The room becomes a blur of activity around me as I focus on my counting, trying desperately to ignore this energy swirling around me. It becomes stronger with each passing second. I ignore him, but he persists with his request for all of us to stop trying to revive him. I let him know that laws prevent me from stopping CPR until the doctor specifically gives that directive. This entire invisible conversation takes place quietly in my mind. It seems I'm the only one to hear this man's silent voice through an instantaneous transfer of thoughts from him to me and back again.

The doctor calls a momentary halt to see what the man's heart is going to do. Everyone holds their collective breath as we wait, hoping to see a blip on the heart monitor. As the doctor and nurses intently stare at the small screen, I sense the man and his thoughts with ever-increasing intensity. A steady stream of energy now flows from him instead of short bursts of thoughts, pictures or words. I feel his readiness to leave, and I remind him there is nothing I can or will do to hasten his departure.

The doctor decides to give the patient one more try, turns to me, and gives me the nod.

The man is ready to "cross over," but the EMT side triumphs once again, and I start chest compressions. I continue until I start to sweat and slow down a bit.

The doctor suddenly halts all activities and stares at the squiggly lines on the monitor. Nothing. No activity at all. The doctor calls for the time, and finally pronounces the man dead. All activity stops in the curtained-off area of the emergency room.

ER team members let out deep sighs. They think they've failed. It becomes personal for them, especially on Christmas Eve. I turn to walk away as cleanup crews hurry to make the room ready for the next patient.

Andrea is in a small family room adjacent to the ER, searching through the bag we brought to the hospital, containing all of the patient's personal effects. We discover his name is "Jack" but can't find a single bit of information about his family or friends. It's important for us to let them know of his passing. Andrea finds a phone number for his place of employment, however, and gives them a call. She informs the boss that Jack will no longer be coming into work, and she asks if Jack has any family or friends for us to contact. She's told that Jack never mentioned any family, and that no one is listed as an emergency contact on his job application.

As I sit next to Andrea and listen to my partner deliver the sad news, I feel a cool burst of energetic air again. I'm pretty sure I know who it's going to be, but in an ER ward I can never be sure until they identify themselves.

It's Jack.

He says he knew he was going to cross over soon, so he had contacted his people a few weeks ago. He says the phone conversations didn't go well, and that they didn't part on good terms. He jokes by saying that maybe he shouldn't have started the contact with a "collect" phone call. He describes himself as being much like the handcuffed man in the next room.

I don't get a chance to ask how he knows there *is* a handcuffed man in the next room before I'm bombarded with feelings of regret and sadness. Jack communicates to me that he walked away from his family. He never followed through on his responsibilities to his children. He now wishes he could have changed his actions, but those kids grew up just fine without him. Jack has no one to say good-bye to, so he tells me I must warn the man in the next room not to waste his chances to be really happy, and that it's never too late to change while there is still a breath in your body.

I tell Jack to go toward the love and light, and that there will be someone there to greet him. He'll be able to keep an eye on his loved ones where he's going. I wish him Godspeed.

Wandering through the ER, I walk past the handcuffed man and feel compelled to turn around. I go back and speak to the officer, knowing the prisoner/patient is listening. I make sure my voice is loud and clear. I share with the officer how sad it is to see someone lose contact with his family and end up dying all alone. Sadder still, no one will know that a family member is no longer on this Earth. Death ends the chances fathers and children have to make amends in this world. I mention that it's never too late while still alive, as long as the heart is involved. The officer shakes her head and says she sees it far too often. We nod in agreement and glance at her prisoner. The man continues to pretend to be asleep.

I hope our conversation left him with a personal wake-up call.

I hear Andrea coming down the hall, so I call out to her. We head out of the hospital and toward our van, walking side by side, not saying a word. It was a tough call for both of us. No one should die all alone, with no family or loved one to hold their hand in comfort, no one to celebrate his or her life, and no one to mourn the loss. We just sit in the van for a few minutes while Andrea busies herself with paperwork. We both take a deep breath, push the Available on Radio (AOR) button, and drive off with no particular destination.

As we drive, I want to share my experience with Andrea and tell her more about Jack. But I back off because I'm afraid she might not understand. We drive in silence, watching last-minute holiday shoppers in a hurry to dash, grab and wrap that one last present.

Our solitude doesn't last long. In less than ten minutes, we're off to another code.

2
Holidays and Halos

As we wind our way through the busy holiday streets, filled with last-minute shoppers, I wonder what will greet us at the next call.

It's easy to find the house because a big red fire truck is parked in front of it, with lights still flashing. I see neighbors milling around outside, curiously looking toward the fire truck. I park the van and look at my partner as I pull on the latex gloves. Andrea grabs her clipboard, along with a library of pamphlets about grief counseling, pushes the "on-scene" computer button, and gives me a smile as we leave the quiet seclusion of our van.

As we approach the residence, I see a young lady outside, pacing back and forth, her arms across her stomach—a sign that trouble is close by. Near the side door, I see an older gentleman sitting with his head in his hands—another sign that this isn't going to be a good day for this family.

I open the side door. The oven heat and aromas from the soon-to-be-ready family dinner blast hot air past me from the small kitchen. This warmth is a welcome omen in place of the cold air I expect to feel on this kind of call.

The fire captain sees us and makes his way over. He starts to fill us in on the details. Quickly and to the point he says, "Wife has cancer. Put on Hospice one week ago. We don't expect to revive her."

He turns to go back into the room where his crew is making its best effort. I see through the crack in the partially open door that the medics are doing CPR on a tiny woman. I sense what will follow all too soon.

Kids run through the kitchen, oblivious to what's going on just a few feet from them, behind that closed door. A cute young boy with an infectious smile approaches me. He wants to know who I am and what I'm doing.

It's then that I feel the cool, energetic breeze enter the room. A faint voice tells me that the young man in front of me is a hellion, but a favorite of the patient's. I know now that she isn't going to be revived. She tells me she wants to go to her Lord and be at peace. She loves her family and will miss them dearly, but she's ready to go.

She tells me her passing will be the hardest on her older son. She wants to know if I can break the news to him in a gentle way. I assure her that I'll do my best and I bid her peace, as she needs to go to the light now. She lets me know she wants to stay a bit longer to see her family through the holiday season. I tell her that it may be painful for her not to, that I understand her desire, and I wish her Godspeed on her journey.

The medics are still in the other room, doing CPR and injecting drugs into her small body. She wants me to tell them to stop, and to thank them for all their wonderful efforts. I think for a moment about passing on that message, and then I erase it from my mind.

Two more grandchildren enter the kitchen. I feel the love she has for all of them. It permeates every corner of this house.

It's getting crowded in the kitchen, so I let my partner know I'm stepping outside to check on other family members. I try to get information from the husband: the man slumped outside the house. He has that "deer in the headlights" stare in his eyes. What I say to him isn't sinking in, and he continues to stare off into the distance as I try to gather information.

The captain comes outside to let me know that the woman has died. The firefighters are packing up and getting ready to go "available" for the next waiting call. More relatives begin to pull up in their cars, expecting a nice family dinner, only to see fire trucks and police cars in front of the house. I see the panic on their faces as they get out of their cars. They want to rush past me, but I stop them. I ask their relation to the family. They're the woman's children. It's now on my shoulders to deliver the news that will stay with them the rest of their lives.

The words flow as they have hundreds of times before.

"Sir, ma'am, my name is Sherri and I'm with the Phoenix Fire Department. I'm sorry to inform you that your Mother has passed away."

The emotions and actions following those words are always a surprise to me. Some people stay calm, trying to reassure me as if *I'm* the one who's grieving. Others fall apart, shrieking, screaming and wailing as if I'm a referee and have the authority to change the game call if they object loudly enough. Most fall somewhere in between.

We're on scene to assist police and family members for over an hour with calls to the doctor's office, coroner's office, mortuary, and out-of-state family members. Once we receive official word that the doctor will sign off on the death certificate, we call the mortuary to pick up the body. When the mortuary staff arrives, Andrea and I distract family and friends so they don't see their loved one leave the house in a body bag. No matter how professionally, respectfully and lovingly this milestone is handled, the body bag is an exceedingly harsh memory to erase during the grieving process.

After the mortuary personnel leave, we ask the husband, sons, and daughters if they have any questions. As my partner answers their inquiries, I feel the cool air fill the space around me once again. Their mother wants me to tell the family she really would have liked the warm, fuzzy bathrobe and slippers they got for her, and she wants them to enjoy the holiday and support each other.

I have to tell her that I'm sorry, and that I can't pass that information along to them because I'm not here in that capacity. She lets me know she understands, but she'd really like them to know of her love for them. I assure her they are very aware of her love, and I'll do what I can to comfort her family.

Before we leave, we hand out Fire Department teddy bears

and stickers to the grandkids. As we wish them a happy holiday. I feel their grandmother close to them. Andrea gives them our bereavement information, containing helpful suggestions for getting through this time of family crisis. It also lists local contact numbers for grief counselors if they feel the need to talk to a professional. We again express our heartfelt sympathies and turn to leave. I feel the deceased close by, and I tell her that she can choose to go to the light or to stay for awhile. It's up to her.

I again wish her Godspeed as we walk out the door.

We climb back into our van and hit our "available" button to let the alarm room know we're ready for another call. As Andrea begins the required paperwork, my thoughts wander.

"How and why did I get into this in the first place?"

My mind hasn't traveled too far down that philosophical memory lane when it's jolted back to reality by the tones going off and the mention of CR 16, our unit. We're instructed to proceed to a location a few miles away to what sounds like a non-traditional medical call.

We pull up to the front of a house, where another fire captain awaits. He's just shaking his head with that smile I've come to recognize as meaning, "this is going to be a doosy!" The captain informs us that this is a couple of "repeat flyers" who have been married for fifty years and have hated each other for forty-nine and a half of those years.

The term "repeat flyer" is used when someone repeatedly calls emergency services for non-emergency events. Some may only call a few times a month, but others call daily. Andrea and I stand there, looking at each other. I motion for her to go first. After all, she's the "green shirt," the more touchy-feely person who does all the talking and counseling on calls like this. Since it's not a medical situation, she's the main contact person.

As we enter the older home, we can hear the couple arguing. She's leaning on a walker, yelling at her husband, and he's all stooped over, shuffling toward the back door. We decide to "divide and conquer." Andrea takes the wife while I follow hubby into the back yard. We listen to both sides of the story, then we get together to compare notes.

This is a "six-of-one-and-a-half-dozen-of-the-other" kind of call. At first check, they both seem to have an onset of dementia. When I tune into the situation, my head spins with confusion. I feel that they both have medical problems, but there's no one who will listen to them anymore. They have joined the ranks of our throw-away elders.

The wife reminds us that her husband has been diagnosed with dementia and that she's the one who's just fine. She says he hides her medicines and won't leave her alone so she can have some peace and quiet in the house. The husband says she hides her own medicines and forgets where she puts them. Neighbors standing outside the front door tell us this has been going on for years.

We can help them find the right agencies to assist them, but I can't help feeling that if they had a better support system, they would be in a better frame of mind and have a better quality of life. The house is filled with confused energy that weighs so heavily that I feel like I'm trying to tap dance through thick tar. I decide to step out into the back yard again to talk to the husband. Besides, it is easier to breathe away from all that swirling, negative energy! It's another example of the fun side-effects of being a psychic-intuitive in my line of work.

Andrea makes very little, if any, headway after ninety minutes of talking and listening to the wife. I eventually decide that we need to get back to the streets, so I inform the elderly lady that we have other calls waiting for us. She continues to repeat her stories but at a higher pitch and faster pace, stories we've now heard over six times since arriving. I quietly but firmly cut her off by explaining that we have phone numbers of people who would be happy to listen to her problems and try to solve them for her. Andrea leaves the lady with lots of helpful information and numbers of agencies she can call once the holiday season is over.

This doesn't satisfy the wife because she wants someone to listen to her "vent" face to face. We finally escape to the sanity of our van.

Calls like this let me feel the inner confusion in some people's minds. I hear their thoughts as they ramble along. At times, their thoughts come in crystal clear, while at other times they're like fuzzy radio signals all scrambled up. Andrea and I agree there's little we can do to assist this couple today. I wish there were some way medical knowledge and services could physically make a difference on this type of call.

I know the man will not live much longer because his aura and energy field are getting very dim. I also know that when he passes, she won't be happy with her life. Sadly, it seems to be playing out just as she expects it will.

We climb into our van and let out deep sighs of frustration. We can't make this emotional call for help better or fix the people in that house. We just hope we don't have to come back out again today. Andrea hits the "available" button and starts on her endless paperwork. As I drive around the city waiting for our next call, we catch up on each other's lives and talk about how far we've come since that first training class.

All this excitement and it's only lunchtime!

3
Getting Started

How did I get started with all this? Well, I'm not really sure. There are times in life when synchronicity just takes over and works its magic on us mere mortals. I'm no exception.

One day, while sitting at my computer, I decided to do a web search for volunteer positions in the City of Phoenix. I found the city's website and a page for volunteer opportunities, clicked on it, and found that the Fire Department needed volunteers. After reading the description of available positions, and what they were looking for in a volunteer, I decided to give it a try. I filled out the form and emailed it in.

As I tapped the "send" button, I had visions of the 1970s television series *Emergency*, about two firefighter-paramedics, Johnny Gage and Roy DeSoto, who saved lives and had great rescue adventures.

A few days later I received a reply. In my mailbox was a huge packet of information to fill out and return to City Hall. If any of the various Fire Department programs were interested in me, they would schedule an interview. A few weeks later, I was asked to interview with the Crisis Response Team personnel.

On the day of the interview, I sat outside a big conference room and listened to muffled voices coming from the other side of the wall. Other interviewees sat, tensely awaiting their turns. As each one left our ranks and disappeared into the conference room, I could feel the tension left in the air from previous hopefuls. The door opened, and a young lady exited, walking past me in a hurry. I was next.

The lady motioned me into the room, where I found myself facing four people: the Review Board. They were going to ask me all kinds of questions to which I had never given much thought.

What were my hobbies? How did I handle stress? What did I do to relax? Oh, and the tough one that could make or break me was, "Suppose you're on the scene of a child drowning.

The parents are so distraught that they don't want to talk to you. They ask you to leave. You have important coping information to give to them. What do you do?"

I later found out that how you answered that question was a big deciding point as to whether you made the team or not. (Sorry: I'm not going to give you the correct answer, in order to protect the integrity of the interview process!)

I sweated out the answers to the tough, but short and simple, questions and answered them honestly. The Review Board members said they would get in touch with me one way or another within a few weeks. Only a week later I received the acceptance letter in the mail. Then came the ninety hours of intense training, with about twenty of us in the class.

A few of us still volunteer and still keep in touch with each other. Andrea, the Lake Havasu resident; Carole, the ex-body builder; Ralph, the retired firefighter; Alton, the firefighter hopeful, and I still keep in close contact. We still laugh about celebrating together after making it through that grueling training course. We knew that what was ahead of us -- the lives we would touch, the drama we would see firsthand, and the stories we would share afterward — would change our lives.

We couldn't have begun to know the intensity and frailty of the human condition. We were all a bit nervous, but anticipation and excitement filled the night air as we sat around the small table, sharing hopes and fears for this new step we were taking together.

With classroom training complete and uniform shirts ordered, we were ready to start our observation rides. At first we watched and shadowed the Crisis Response Team as they handled the calls.

As I said earlier, each team consists of a blue-shirted emergency medical technician (EMT) and a green-shirted behavioral health specialist (BHS). The twenty-foot Fire Department van is fully equipped to handle most emergencies we encounter while on a call. The equipment consists of an Automatic External Defibrillator (AED), oxygen, medical kits, car seats, baby supplies, a cooler with ice water, and donated sports drinks, maps, road hazard-safety warning equipment, two-way radios, a laptop computer, blankets, coloring books and crayons, trauma teddy bears, and a file cabinet for our library of pamphlets covering most of the situations we handle.

A shift is either a twelve- or twenty-four hour day, and we stay at a fire station for meals and sleep. We're required to volunteer either two twelve-hour shifts or one twenty-four hour shift each month.

Retired Phoenix Fire Chief Alan Brunacini started the Alternative Response Program, later renamed Crisis Response Team (CRT), many years ago. He said that when the house fire was over and the engines pulled away, he was saddened by the families left behind who had no idea what to do next. Being a great humanitarian, he decided he needed to do something more. The Alternative Response Program was born.

The CRTs responds to codes, gunshots, stabbings, drownings, family crises and coping problems, death notifications...anything that combines "trauma with drama," as we put it. It's said the CRTs go "where angels fear to tread." I wouldn't go that far, because I rarely see any angels; unless you count firefighters.

When I started, I wasn't aware that I'd be communicating with dead people, or that my intuitive skills would come into play. I just thought it would be interesting to assist my community. Imagine my surprise when I started responding to calls and got way more than I bargained for!

My first few shifts were uneventful but rewarding. I was just getting the hang of it when, one night, it all changed. The summons came through as a "Crisis Care" call.

We had to inform a mother of three young children that her husband had committed suicide. I was the "green shirt" on this one, so I had to do all the talking. My EMT was there for support and medical backup, if needed, once the family was informed. This would be my first death notification, and was I nervous!

As we drove to the location, I rehearsed over and over in my mind what I would say. We pulled up to the house, and I just sat in the van, not sure if I wanted to get out. My EMT looked over and reassured me that I could do it. We approached the door and knocked. A lady answered. We asked if we could come in for a moment to talk with her, and she invited us in. It was a simple house: clean, well kept, and with lots of family pictures on the walls - the normal trappings of a happy family.

I learned quickly that what you see on the surface doesn't always represent what lies beneath.

The wife knew something was very wrong, and that we weren't there to talk about smoke alarms and water safety. I asked if she knew where her husband was at that moment, and she shook her head. She confided they'd had a big argument and scuffle the night before. She'd called the police but he left before they got there, and hadn't come home.

I knew he wouldn't be coming home because he'd shot himself in the head on a dark street in the middle of the night while listening to his truck radio.

I started my speech: "Ma'am, my name is Sherri and I'm with the Phoenix Fire Department. I'm sorry to inform you that your husband has passed away." I dropped the bomb and waited for the reaction.

The wife started crying, repeating, "no, no, no!" over and over. She said there had to be some kind of mistake. She wanted to know how, when, and where it happened. I think she expected to hear me say her husband was murdered, but I sat her down, looked her in the eyes and told her the truth. I told her he was found dead in his truck late the night before, after people heard a gunshot and called the police.

Her next question was who murdered him. She was sure he wouldn't commit suicide. I handed her a few tissues, then waited for her to wipe her face and blow her nose.

It took a moment to sink in that this whole thing was not some kind of cruel joke on her. I told her again that it had been ruled a suicide by the police because of evidence found at the scene. She insisted again that he would never do such a thing to them or to himself; that he loved her and his kids. That I had to be wrong! I assured her that I wasn't. She resumed crying with intermittent sobs like hiccups. I handed her more tissues.

Then the woman left the room and grabbed the phone, as if to prove me wrong. I just sat and waited for her to return, and I could hear her speaking on the phone from the adjoining room.

I started to tune out all the surrounding noise and go into a zone, a quiet place where there is just peace. I tried to stay in that place for a moment because I had a strange feeling that all hell was about to break loose, and I couldn't figure out why, or where the feeling was coming from. I've learned not to ignore these feelings, so I put my feelers out and paid attention to what was going on around me.

While standing in the living room, I got a very odd feeling, one of uneasiness and discontentment. I started to pace, and got a feeling of being very out of place and confused. A cool rush of air swirled around me, followed by a "hair on the arm raising" feeling. I looked for the cause of the draft but couldn't find one. Thoughts raced through my head as I tried to think of how I was going to inform the children that their father was dead. They would be home from school shortly.

I looked at their family pictures on the wall, and saw a picture of their dad. I could almost hear him talking in my head. His voice came through like a radio station not quite tuned in. I thought that maybe the stress was already starting to get to me, and I tried to shake it off. It returned, just as loud and persistent. I looked around. There were only the three of us in the house, my partner, the wife, and I; but I couldn't shake the feeling that someone was watching me.

The wife came back into the room, crying harder than before. She no longer insisted that I was wrong about her husband. She paced, still quietly sobbing. She said he was a good husband and a great father. As she spoke, I heard that voice in my head again. The voice told me that he was *not* a good husband. He cheated on her, lied to her, and was known to hit her for no reason. He said he was a good dad though. He loved his kids, and he was sorry for what he'd done in a moment of weakness, frustration and anger. He wanted revenge, to see her suffer; but he never really thought it through. He was saddened by what he'd done and wanted to change everything.

I listened to all of this with awe. No one else in the room seemed to hear and feel what I was hearing and feeling. The room began to feel cooler and electrified, with energy running rampant through the room and right into me. I decided to get out of there for a minute, so I stepped outside to get some fresh air and drinking water from the van.

I opened the back doors of the van and reached right to the ice chest. I shoved the water bottles out of the way and splashed some cold ice water on my face.

"That should wake me up and clear my head," I thought.

I stood there for a minute, trying to figure out what had gone on inside that house. I heard nothing in my head anymore, so it must have been an overactive imagination. I grabbed a few bottles of water and headed back into the house.

Immediately upon entering, I felt that cool sensation again. This time, I told myself, it was because of the ice water from the cooler outside; not to worry. I handed water bottles to everyone and sat back down. The wife was still crying, and the pile of tissues next to her was getting bigger and bigger. We needed to find out how she wanted us to tell her kids, who would be walking through the door any minute. As I looked up at their pictures, I heard that voice in my head again.

It was going to be a very strange day.

The voice was adamant that the children not be told. He'd made a mistake. He wanted to come back. If I told the kids the truth, he would have no hope left. The voice begged me not to tell the kids of his death. He insisted that he would find a way back, that I just give him some time!

I seriously considered my state of mind. I'd already gone on calls where patients needed assistance because they heard voices.

"Great," I thought to myself, "now I'm going to be one of them. Now *I'm* a '918'!" (That's the police code for a mentally unstable person.)

I decided there was only one logical thing to do, so I asked the voice in my mind, "Who's talking to me, and why am I hearing you?"

The voice explained that he was talking to me because I was the only one listening. No one else had been able to hear him. He tried talking to his wife, brother, and a few cousins, but I was the only one who heard him. He tried talking to the police officers and the medical crews at the scene, but no one would listen. He was confused about what was happening to him, and he was desperate.

He pleaded with me to give his family his messages; he said he had so many things to say and to make amends for. I told him I couldn't give that kind of information to his wife or kids, that I had to fulfill my own job requirements, and that passing information from deceased loved ones wasn't in the job description! He ignored this, and persisted in telling me what to say.

This was all new to me, and I felt helpless and frustrated. I wrestled with the decision and decided not to pass on his information. As it was, I walked a fine line doing my job, and I didn't want to step on the wrong side of it. I did let the wife know there was a team of specialized personnel coming to help her with informing the children about their father's passing. They would be able to help the kids deal with the tragedy on a long-term basis.

Even then I felt the father's fears, and he emphatically repeated that he did not want the kids told. I reminded him that they must be told. For lack of anything else to say, I suggested that he go to the children in their dreams and let them know that he still loved them. Kids, I knew, seem to sense energies better than most adults.

Once the new team arrived, we headed back out to our van. I went straight to the chest of ice water. It didn't offer much comfort, but it gave me something else, something physical, to think about. How could I explain this call, this experience, to anyone? I decided to stay mum and hope it wouldn't happen again.

We arrived at our fire station and made our way to the small office where we finish paperwork. I filed it away and headed for one of the large recliners in the TV room. I found myself in a state of shock. I wanted to get away; I felt like running out the station door and never looking back!

Feeling other people's thoughts wasn't unusual because it had happened to me before. It usually happened when someone was physically too close to me, like in a crowded theater or at a nightclub.

Being an intuitive isn't easy because "turning it off" is tough. I'm able to tell people about their thoughts, emotions and actions before I even know their names. You'd think that with those abilities I would have made better choices in my own life! Go figure.

Throughout life I had tried to ignore these odd insights. I could have made much better choices in life had I "tuned in" and listened to my inner voice instead of running away and ignoring those feelings. It wasn't until I decided to accept the opportunity and responsibility of it all that I found the love of my life, my husband, Yale.

What a treasure he is! I met him in a nightclub one evening. By this point in my dating life, I'd devised three questions to ask potential mates. I was able to tune into their thoughts and get the real answers to my questions. Yale answered the questions perfectly, and he gained my attention on a deeper level.

Ladies, here are the questions you should ask all potential mates: (1) *When is your mother's birthday?* This denotes a softer side and is a signal that they will most likely remember your important days. (2) *What was the last book you read?* This lets you know they're learning and growing. And finally, (3) *What do you do on a typical Sunday?* If they go to church and then watch sports, and you don't like either, then start looking elsewhere. My daughter, Becky, found a great husband using those questions. Dustin is a real keeper, and I'm proud of both of them.

Going out in public is tough on those of us who are very sensitive to the energies of others. When I was small, my mother always told me that I had an overactive imagination. Stray dogs and cats would follow me home and become my new best friends. I didn't realize then that not everyone could communicate with animals. I could sense what they wanted or needed. I held great conversations with my many pets as a child. Making real friends was easy for me. Keeping them was a different story.

Not everyone wants to know that you can tell them what

they're thinking or feeling. Throughout the stages of my life, I would pick one or two friends and just hang out with them. Being in crowds would make me jumpy or edgy. and then very tired. As I grew older, I limited myself to the people I would share my life with. I became reclusive.

That all changed one day, thanks to a fateful car accident and a letter I received in the mail.

4
China

Some years ago I was rear-ended in a car accident, experienced severe whiplash, and went to a local chiropractor for adjustments. After a few weeks, he said I was improving, but that it would be great if I could get a few massages to alleviate the muscle tightness. I lived in a very small town in Wisconsin, and there were no such creature comforts within fifty miles. The chiropractor suggested I attend massage school, then he would hire me to work for him.

I checked around for massage schools, and I found one in Milwaukee, a good two-and-a-half hour drive away. I'd be attending school during the winter while the snow flew and temperatures were below zero on a warm day. After months of spending four days a week living in a large, four-story co-op house in Milwaukee and driving back to my home town on weekends, I graduated.

I started working for the chiropractor, but I soon discovered that it was better to be my own boss and set my own hours. I opened a small office in a building right on Main Street and "put out my shingle." Customers came more out of curiosity than need. Many people had never experienced a professional massage and wanted to be the first to get one. I noticed that as I focused on the person lying on my massage table, I could sense what was wrong with him or her, and that I would be able to assist much more easily.

Word got out, as it does in most small towns, and I became very busy. As I worked on my clients, they would ask me questions and I would give them "insights" as I called them. My clients were always surprised, and they wondered how I knew such personal things. All I had to do was get within three feet of them and information would just start pouring into me. Sometimes it was a loved one who had crossed over who wanted to give them a message, and sometimes it was something they were worrying about for which I could provide a solution.

I started to work with the local high school sports teams because my son, Michael, played sports and was complaining of muscle tightness. I made a deal with the basketball coach to volunteer my time to work with the students if he gave me free advertising in the program that was handed out at every game.

It turned out very well for all of us! Soon I was working with a pro-sports minor league team, and eventually with some of their big-name baseball counterparts. I knew I could help with physical injuries, but wanted to do more. The answer was buried somewhere in my brain, if only I could reach it.

Around this time, I signed up for a meditation class. I didn't know what to expect, but it sounded interesting even though it meant driving for an hour. But after my first class, I was hooked. Anna May Cottrell was the guide and master of this class. Anna May channeled during most of the sessions, which I found fascinating. Simply put, channeling is allowing a higher form of communication to talk or act through you. I learned so much there and gained such insight regarding a side of life I never knew existed!

After a few months attending her weekly classes, Anna May's spirit guides informed me that I would be off on a great adventure over a vast body of water. Well, I'm from Wisconsin and my family has never traveled far from home, so I didn't take this as seriously as I should have. Perhaps I was going to Michigan, across the Great Lakes. Never did I dream it meant going over an ocean.

I continued my practice and volunteered time working with the International Olympic Committee throughout the Midwestern United States and Canada, doing massage on team members from around the world. After one of those sessions, I arrived home, picked up the mail, and began sifting through the junk mail before heading back up the long driveway. After becoming nationally certified in massage therapy, I received daily junk mail asking me to join this or buy that. Sometimes it was entertaining, so I put the junk mail on the table and gave it no more thought.

Later that evening I browsed through the mail to see what was being offered that week. I came

The author with Master Wang Juemin

across a letter inviting me to train in Beijing, China, at the Olympic Training Center.

"Wow," I thought, "I wonder how much that would cost me?" Not having extra cash, I set it aside with the rest of the junk mail.

A few days later I received a call from a lady asking me if I was interested in going to China. The cutoff date to accept was fast approaching, and they needed to fill that spot. I explained to her that I received the letter but had no money to pay for a trip to China anytime soon. She said I'd made a mistake: This was an all-expenses-paid invitation.

I was no sophisticate from New York City, but I did know that nothing in life is free. We talked for a while as she tried to convince me to accept the offer. It was a round-trip to and from Beijing and included hotel accommodations, training with elite instructors, and two meals a day for six weeks. There would be twenty of us flying to the Olympic Training Center to be instructed in *Twaina*, an ancient sports-massage technique. I told her I'd think about it and call her the next day.

I went to my parents' home and asked them what they thought of this offer. My mother is also a bit of an intuitive herself, so I wanted her opinion. They reminded me that nothing in life was free, but that a chance like this didn't come along everyday. I was tossing and turning all night trying to make up my mind when I remembered what Anna May had told me. Maybe this was for me after all. I decided to go for whatever this experience had to offer.

After all, what could possibly go wrong?

A few short weeks later, I was flying over a large body of water to a life-milestone destiny.

Training in Beijing was incredible. The sights, smells, food and throngs of people filled me with awe. Because it was less than a year after the Tiananmen Square protests of 1989, we were assigned official guides and couldn't travel without them. Most of the people we met were very friendly and very curious about us, as we were about them.

Toward the end of my fifth week, we were introduced to a master of *Qigong*, a 4,000 year-old Chinese secret until just recently. It's an advanced form of energy healing much like Reiki, only more powerful. Master Wang Juemin was going to teach us how to keep our energy strong and not become drained as we worked on people.

As we sat in meditation that day, he had one of his trained viewers scan each of us to see what they could see. The "viewers" are able to see into the body and detect where *chi*, or energy, might be stuck. Senders of *chi* can then move that energy and assist in healing the person. I was informed that I was very lucky indeed as I was able to do both, send and see. I was told that very few people have the ability to do both. I was excited because I knew that these new skills would be able to help in my work back home.

At the end of one very long day, Master Wang approached me with his interpreter and asked if I would like to train with him. At the time, I didn't grasp what an honor this was for me. We only had one more week on the schedule, and part of that would be a very long, bumpy bus ride to see some ancient *terra cotta* warrior statues. Learning *Qigong* sounded far more interesting, so I agreed to stay and train with Master Wang. I didn't know exactly what I had agreed to, as the language barrier was as solid as the Great Wall that day.

I soon found out that I would be staying for a few more months, not just a few more days. I was equally nervous, scared and excited about this new adventure. My nineteen new friends would leave me behind to fly back home, while I would stay in a strange country all by myself. I spoke very little Chinese: "May I have some water?" "Where's the bathroom?" and that was about it. Not a bad beginning, but definitely not stand-on-your-own conversation-starters!

I boarded an old steam train with Master Wang and his assistants, and off into the blue we traveled. It took a few hours to get to Master Wang's Qigong Hospital in Boading. An assistant to Master Wang named Master Li, and his wife, adopted me for the duration of my stay. Morning started early, and "sleeping in" was unheard of. So were cable TV and computers, by the look of things.

I wondered what I was going to do with my free time, but I soon found that there was no such thing. I spent many long hours every day in training with Master Wang or one of his assistants. Master Wang told me that he was going to awaken ancient memories within me, and I eagerly accepted. He explained that I had lived many lifetimes as a healer, and he was going to assist me in remembering who I was and what I was capable of doing. I agreed, not knowing what this would entail.

Master Wang took me under his wing, and his assistant, Master Li, made sure I did my studies every day. I learned about the energy the Chinese call *chi*. *Chi* is all around us, and we can learn to harness it for so many wonderful things. Master Wang tried to show me, by his example, how energy around people could change from one thought to the next. I was trying so hard, but I wasn't catching on to this *chi* thing.

Then, one day after a session of meditation, I started noticing colors around people. I sat and just watched as they swirled about the students while they meditated. Master Wang noticed what I was doing and decided to fully open my "third eye" *chakra* (energy center) for me. He said I would progress much faster and further into knowing who I was.

That wasn't as much fun as I thought it would be! I was bombarded by visions, colors, thoughts and emotions all at once. Everything became much more multi-dimensional, like wearing a pair of 3-D glasses. Now I could truly appreciate Shirley MacLaine and her best-selling book *Out on a Limb* even more.

I just never thought it would happen to me.

Qigong is used to heal numerous illnesses. I was there in the courtyard one afternoon when an older man with a very young teenage girl arrived. They had traveled for many weeks to get to the Qigong Hospital and had faced many hardships along the way. The father brought his daughter to Master Wang so he might heal her eyesight. She was almost blind, and glasses could no longer correct her vision. This was tragic for the family as the young girl couldn't work, and the parents wouldn't be able to marry her off when the time came. She would become a burden to her family in the near future.

Master Wang was expecting them, and he started sessions right away. He started moving his own *chi* through his body, then started to send it into the young girl's body. A minute or two went by; I waited to see what would happen. I wondered if maybe nothing was going to happen — until Master Li came up behind me and reminded me to look with my "third eye" and not my physical eyes. When I did, everything became like one of those Magic Eye™ posters you stare at until suddenly a picture appears out of the chaos!

I saw the energy as it entered the girl and wound its way through her body, taking the path of least resistance like a lava flow. After about five minutes, I noticed the young girl's body start to twitch. Her whole body looked and acted as though she were going into seizures. Some of the assistants moved her to the ground, and then Master Wang really went to work.

It was as though she had no control over her body. Her arms and legs jerked and shuddered simultaneously in multiple directions. This lasted about ten minutes before Master Wang stopped to give the young girl a rest.

These sessions went on for a number of weeks while I was there. The girl's eyesight improved a great deal before they finally had to leave the hospital and make their way home. I was told that many people wait years to be seen by Master Wang, and they make great sacrifices to reach Boading. This family stayed in a very small room, where they cooked, ate, slept and used a chamber pot, just like everyone else who comes to be healed.

I finished my training time with Master Wang, and I was very sad to leave. I packed my bags, and the many small presents from my new friends, and said my goodbyes. I boarded a plane to come home a very different person than the one who had left a few short months before.

Master Wang said I was "a real *Qigong* master now." Then he added, "Again!"

I now knew how to assist in healing injuries and move trapped *chi* - even from a distance - to bring about profound changes in people. What I did with that knowledge was going to be totally up to me.

5
Into Practice

I immediately began to practice what I'd learned.

While headed home on the plane, the lady next to me complained of a headache. I used my newfound skills in *Qigong* to ease the throbbing. Word soon spread among the passengers that I could heal things. After all, we were in the air for half a day, and chatting with people seemed to be the thing to do. As the hours went by, passengers lined up for my assistance. I could see where the injury was before they told me, and I would send the *chi* flowing out. First it would get very hot, then settle down to a warm sensation.

I collected quite a few tips on that flight. I was even allowed into the cockpit to work on the pilot and co-pilot during our long journey.

Once back home, I fully expected to be excited about getting back to my normal life. Surprisingly, I found that I missed China and all the wonders it held. To balance the emptiness, I decided to practice what I'd learned, so I advertised my new modality of *Qigong*, along with my usual massage practice. After working on a few patients, word got out, just like on that plane, and I was swamped with calls. Before long, professional athletes were calling. That was when my son, Michael, decided that he needed to be my new office assistant. Our deal was that he would answer the phone, make the appointments, and help out with accounting, and he could keep the autographs. It worked out great for both of us!

Business expanded, and I was traveling around the Midwest working on minor-league athletes and staying in hotels. I met many of the up-and-coming sports stars, and some who were on their way down. They started to place their career hopes on my abilities, and the pressure grew.

One day I got a call from a major sports team owner asking if I would come to Phoenix during spring training. Anything that could take me away from four feet of snow sounded great. I agreed.

It was arranged for me to be in Phoenix for three months, so I loaded up my car, and off I went. Once again I was headed for unknown realms. I never thought of myself as adventurous, but once my mind opened, everything else opened along with it. I found a cozy, two-bedroom apartment and began seeing my assigned clientele, many of whom were very well known.

It was a bit unnerving to work on them, but they made me feel so at ease! I found that my skills could assist athlete in healing twice as fast as other methods. I was now in big demand, and my career was taking off.

With success came greed, and I'm sorry to say that I toppled into its clutches. My practice became all about the money, and not about helping people, forsaking the life I had agreed to honor as a healer.

It was then that tragedy struck. A huge athlete was lying on my massage table when he started to roll over, but he was in the wrong position, and started to go over the edge! Instinct took over, and I reached out and grabbed for him. As I did, I felt a sharp, burning pain in my shoulder. It was dislocated, and I myself was "sidelined"!

Two surgeries and months of rehabilitation later, nothing was back to normal. I just wanted to get back to work and to making the big bucks I had become so accustomed to. I later learned that as long as I held that thought, I wouldn't be allowed to return to my work. A downward spiral into depression separated me from my life.

During this period, I met Yale, the man who would become my husband, and his outlook on life saved me. Who would guess that a nuclear engineer would have such deep thoughts about the metaphysical!

Yale listened to my stories, complaints and whining with the "patience of Job." The doctors had me on so many medicines that my mind and intuitive skills had numbed. I realized that "meds" were not all that bad if they blocked those exterior thoughts from invading my mind. I also realized that my life was "on hold," and I didn't seem to care.

It was really Yale's idea for me to get out and become useful to myself again: not to worry about others but to do something that made me happy. He was right in more ways than one.

I put it off until one day in September, when terrorist planes hit New York City's twin towers. I still hear the voices of people as they crossed over, Their voices were so loud and so clear in my head! I knew hundreds of innocent victims crossed over at the same time, and I decided then and there to get on with living my life.

I went back to my parents' home in Wisconsin for a few weeks to take myself off about ten different prescription medications, many of which were interfering with one another and producing all sorts of miserable side effects. My parents were saints, and I was soon flying back home to my husband, medication-free, and ready to begin helping others again.

That is how I came to be with the Phoenix Fire Department, volunteering on the Crisis Response vans.

6
Convincing the Dead

With each CRT call that I'm assigned, I become more aware of the energies that surround all of us. My "sixth sense" is opening wider, and my intuitive abilities are growing stronger. The crisis calls vary from shift to shift, making each one more interesting than the last.

At that original training class, I met Carole, a great partner and friend. She found out about my abilities, and she teases me mercilessly whenever possible. On code calls, she asks me how many people I see so she can compare it with her imaginary list. Our numbers rarely match!

One day a call comes in for a fall injury. This isn't a routine assignment, so it piques our curiosity. As we pull up to the house, I get the distinct smell of horses and a barn. We're in the middle of the city! There's no trace of a farm as far as I can see. When I mention this smell, Carole looks at me strangely and says something about "taking the girl out of the country," but I'm already out of the van. Police cars line the street.

This looks to be much more than a fall injury.

We enter the house, and I see a small man motioning for us to hurry. I turn to tell Carole to follow him, but when I turn again, the small man is gone. I want to say something but put it out of my mind, and we continue through the house into the backyard.

There I see a sheet covering a very small body on the ground. As I survey the yard, not far from the body, I see a ladder going up to the roof. Because of the body's size, I assume it's a child. I ask some of the police officers what happened. They say that he, gesturing toward the body, shot himself while up on the roof, fell off, and landed where he is now. I wonder why a child would have a gun in the first place, never mind on a rooftop!

Suddenly I detect that horse and barn smell again, and I look around to try and pinpoint it. No one is nearby when that cool feeling surrounds me. This can only mean one thing – there's a spirit close by who wants to communicate. I wander through the house trying to make contact with it, and it doesn't take long for us to find each other. As I round the corner, there's a man of very small stature standing in front of me. I blink, and he's gone again.

I decide to go to the backyard to see who's under that sheet.

As I lift the sheet, I see that very man lying there on the ground! It's the same man who motioned to me when we arrived. Okay. That solves that mystery. Now what does he want from me?

I decide to go to the van to get water from the cooler, seemingly my place of refuge while working on these calls. I plunge my hands into the icy water and wet the back of my neck to cool off. I take a deep, cleansing breath, then head back to the house to face what's in there.

As I enter the house, my mind fills with thoughts that I know aren't coming from me. I see horses, a racetrack, brightly colored pajamas, and I smell clean leather. I'm not sure how the PJs got in there, but there they were. There's a feeling of disappointment, longing, and not fitting in with life.

Now I'm baffled. I search for Carole. She's talking with one of the deceased man's friends. I hear them say that he was a jockey at a racetrack for most of his life.

Ah, now it all makes sense! Those weren't PJs but racing silks! The smell of horse gets stronger once I make that connection. It's like I'm being encouraged to keep going.

I talk to the deceased's friends, who have gathered to find out more about what happened to our jockey. They don't know why he would have done something like this. I tell them that perhaps he just felt like he didn't fit in anywhere but the track, and that once he lost that connection, because of his last injury, he felt totally out of place in life.

They suddenly ask how I know about his injuries, and I realize that I've volunteered too much information. I change the subject, and the matter is soon forgotten. We wait until the medical examiner's team arrives to take the body away. As we usher the family out of the room, I feel a cool draft blow past me.

I try to ignore the draft, but my new jockey friend is very insistent that I talk with him. I begin to feel his feelings, and they're very strong: fear and confusion. He's upset that all these people are touching him. He wants to know what they're doing to him and why he can't wake up. He says this is just a bad dream.

How do I convince someone that he's dead? That was never covered in any training class I ever took!

I take a deep breath and begin, "My name is Sherri, and I'm sorry to inform you that you are dead." I drop the bomb, and now I wait for the reaction.

I can feel his disbelief and shock as my words sink in. Confusion swirls in the air as pictures flip quickly by in my mind's eye. I see him recount his actions earlier that day. Realization of what he did hits him and, in a blink of an eye, his energy is gone. I no longer sense him around me. I'm not sure what happened to him, but I hope he found the light and love and headed toward it.

Sometimes the recently departed don't have a message to send on. The shock of their deaths leaves them unable to think while I'm there. Their messages may not come to me during the call, but they've been known to follow me back to the station or even to my home. The jockey was more concerned with his body than with leaving a message. Each soul is different. Personalities continue on even after bodies don't. This soul didn't leave a message for me, and I never heard from him again.

We finish our paperwork and assist the deceased's friends with the steps they will encounter next, and we head for the van. Carole waits until we're a few blocks away before she pulls over.

"What was that all about?" she asks.

How do I even begin to explain? I take a deep breath and start with smelling the horses, then go from there. When I finish, she gives me one of those "you're truly weird" looks and just smiles. Thankfully, the rest of the day is uneventful.

This first open conversation leads to a new routine whenever we're paired as a team. We would meet at my house after each shift to debrief the day's events with each other. I fill Carole in on the behind-the-scenes activities she doesn't get to see. Discussing these soul interceptions with Carole genuinely helps me because she has a great way of bringing me back down to Earth.

Carole still thinks I'm bizarre, but she keeps an open mind and overlooks my weirdness. We talk about each call and how we can improve on anything we did or didn't do. We start talking about what we're going to do for the next few days, with a bit of gossip thrown in. As we talk, tension leaves our bodies, and normalcy returns to both of us.

We say goodnight and go our separate ways, each with a sense of accomplishment.

My next shift is with a partner with whom I have never worked. I'm the "green shirt" on this shift, the "touchy feely" half of the team. We're just starting our shift and checking our van when the call comes across the radio. We're being called out to a 962, a car crash with injuries. The message on the computer says the victim is in a full code, and CPR has been started. All I can think is, "Here we go again, right off the starting blocks."

As we arrive on scene, we put on reflective vests and gloves, flip on our warning lights, and get out of the van. This car crash is in the middle of a busy street during morning rush-hour traffic. As we approach the car, we see the deceased on the ground. Medics are working on him, and his wife is standing close by, crying. We take her aside and ask her what happened. She tells us that she doesn't really know. One minute they were talking about their plans for the day and where to go for breakfast, and the next thing she remembered was the crash and the air bags deploying.

The rescue unit loads the man into the ambulance and races off to the hospital. We offer to take the wife to the hospital. She accepts, and we assist her into the van. The ambulance races ahead with its lights flashing and sirens blaring. We arrive a few minutes behind it. We settle the wife in the waiting area with a nurse and inform her that we'll check on her husband.

Hospitals are hit-or-miss propositions for me. Sometimes I go into a hospital and don't feel the presence of anyone, while at other times I'm bombarded with many who are waiting to cross over. This is one of those busy days for me. I feel many cool spots as we make our way through the maze of rooms in the emergency department. I try to block out the sensations so I can do my job efficiently, but it doesn't always work. Some souls have a very strong energy and push to make their presence known to me. I tell them to go to the light and the love, and that I just can't assist them more at this time.

We find the man from the car accident in bay 2 of the emergency room. There's a team of doctors and nurses working feverishly to bring him back. As my partner and I watch, I feel a coolness surround me. The hairs on my arms begin to rise up. I'm getting better now at realizing what this means, but it isn't getting any easier. I ask who has the message for me and open my senses to wait for the response.

I sense that the man we're there for is trying to get a message to me. He fades in and out for a few minutes. Finally I hear the doctor call out, "Time?" All activity stops. I know this man is now legally dead.

As the ER team goes on to the next emergency, I feel that the man is still here with me. Again I ask him what his message is. I sense his confusion and even feel the tightness in his chest. He lets me know that his heart stopped, and then the accident happened, not the other way around. He's worried about his wife. I reassure him we'll help her. He lets me know that he's no longer in pain and that he feels so much love around him. I tell him I'm going to inform his wife now, and he can go to the light when he's ready.

My partner and I go to the waiting area and ask the wife to join us in a private room. By the look on my face, she knows this is bad, and she starts sobbing before we can even deliver the official news to her. I feel that coolness again as I tell her what happened. I let her know that her husband has passed away and that he didn't suffer. She continues to sob as I hand her tissues to dry her tears.

We sit with her for a few minutes before the EMT decides he needs to check on something and excuses himself. Maybe he feels the extra presence and gets uncomfortable, or maybe he really just wants to check on something. Most of the guys I partner with are not into the "touchy feely" stuff and will "bail" if given half a chance.

The man wants me to give his wife a message, so I tell him I'll try, but give no promises. He says that in the top drawer of his desk at home he has a present waiting for her. It's their anniversary in a few days, and he felt compelled to buy her gift a few days early, not the night before as he usually did.

Now I have to decide if and how I'm going to inform her of this. As we talk for a few minutes, she makes the opening for me in our conversation. She mentions that their anniversary is in a few days, and she doesn't even know where to begin to start canceling their party.

I pat her hand and tell her that we can get through this one moment at a time. I tell her that when she gets home, she should get a pad of paper and write everything she must do to cancel the party arrangements and to assign tasks to other family members. I feel her mind whirling with all her fears. She mentions to me that she has no way to pay the bills if he leaves her now, and she begins to cry even harder. She doesn't want to move from her house because they have so many memories there together. But now she can't afford to make the payments.

I again tell her to sit at their desk at home, to get paper from the top drawer, and just start making a list of things to do. The husband has shown me his desk with the drawer open and the paper with the anniversary card underneath. Inside the card is the deed for their house, and it's marked "Paid In Full."

He was going to surprise her with it on their anniversary!

He also tells me that he invested wisely years ago, so she will be just fine, with no need to worry about money. He shows me a lawyer's business card by the phone. I let her know she should contact their lawyer and that he will be able to assist her with any final details, and answer all her questions. I wait with her until a neighbor comes to get her. I know she'll be fine and that her husband will be watching over her.

I wish I could be there to see her face when she finds that card!

We leave the hospital and all those feelings behind as we settle into our van once again. We make ourselves available to the Alarm Room and wait for the next call.

It won't be long. It never is.

7
Energies

The Alarm Room is the 911 nerve center where all emergency calls go. The room is strangely electrifying, like watching the floor of the New York Stock Exchange from above. It's that sort of firm, low-pitched, controlled chaos with an out-of-control, audible lid on top. Highly trained and experienced dispatchers quickly prioritize calls and send them to the closest available unit for response.

As CRT members, we never know what kind of calls we'll be sent to handle. Some are funny, some sad, some are harder to work than others, but they're always rewarding. Whenever we drive back to the station, we know that the firefighters, who happen to be outstanding cooks, will have a great meal waiting. Even if a call takes us past meal time, we know the firefighters always have plenty to share, and will save some for us whenever we get the chance to get back there to eat it. Granola bars and other goodies are always in my gear bag.

The Alarm Room suddenly alerts us that we're being sent out to assist with a suicidal man.

We pull up to the apartment building and head into the central courtyard to begin our search for the apartment. As we round the corner, it's very clear where we need to be. Three sweaty police officers are standing outside an open apartment door in the summer's blazing heat. Dark uniforms and layers of protective clothing and equipment add to their discomfort. Relief washes over their collective faces when they see us.

We're the cavalry arriving to relieve their watch.

I approach the lead officer and ask him about the situation. He states that the man inside is depressed and has threatened to kill himself. I tune into the energies coming from the apartment, and I don't feel a threat from within, so I peek around the corner and introduce myself. I hear a voice answer but don't see anyone inside. I ask if it's okay to come in. A nice voice answers that I'm welcome, but cops are not.

"Great," I say, "because I'm not a cop. My name is Sherri and I'm with the Fire Department."

I enter the small, darkened apartment. My partner is close behind. Despair and overwhelming depression fall on me like a ton of bricks. The slow-moving energy is stifling and stale. I make my way to the center of the living room and ask if I can meet whoever is in here.

Daniel steps out from a corner, a handsome, Native American man who looks to be in his early thirties. I ask Daniel how I can help. He invites me to sit on a huge pillow on the floor.

We sit face to face and say nothing for a few moments. Daniel then reaches across the empty space and touches my hand. The cops outside the door are ever watchful and vigilant about my safety. They eye Daniel warily.

We hold hands and connect our energies. I can tell by this one action that Daniel is very sensitive to the forces around him. I sit quietly and wait for him to speak. He finally begins. He says he doesn't know what has taken hold of him but, whatever it is, it won't leave him alone. I told him I felt the same thing when I first stepped inside. For the first time, he makes eye contact with me. He's relieved that I'm not here to judge him, but rather to understand and help.

We chat for a few minutes, and he tells me about his life, how he feels like a second-class citizen. I continue to hold his hand and listen. When he finishes, he looks up at me again. I tell him I understand more than he thinks I do, and that there may be a way to get rid of the negative energies, if he wants to try.

Daniel is curious now, and he wants to know how I can do that. I tell him a small part of my story of training in China and about learning to deal with energies. I feel a bond starting to form between us, and I know that he'll be okay if he learns to clear his energy field off every day. I explain to Daniel that when we're sensitive to the energies around us, we must learn to "clear off" every day, and maybe even a few times a day.

I have his undivided attention now. His eyes focus completely on my face. He wants to know how to do this.

Clearing the energy from your aura is much the same as washing your hands. There are several ways I like to use to clear the energy field of junk that I pick up. One way is to just shake my whole body for a minute like a wet dog. By shaking, I send all the negative energies out and off from my body. Another way is to "smudge" my surroundings and myself frequently. Smudging consists of burning sage or cedar, then letting the smoke wash over you. This clears out negative energies and has been used by Native Americans for thousands of years.

I also tell Daniel that he can hum notes or spray special oils around to clear out what he doesn't want in his energy field. The process can be as simple as running your hands under cool water for a few minutes. I remind him to ask that "All things be aligned for his highest good" when he prays or asks for anything.

We discuss different methods for a few more minutes before I ask him the last time he did a "sweat lodge," an ancient Native American spiritual practice. He says it has been many years, but he enjoyed them when he did them. I give him a phone number of a friend who does sweat lodges, and I urge Daniel to give him a call.

Daniel tells me he's grateful and very happy that I don't think he's crazy. He's had people out before, and that was how they treated him. I tell Daniel the energies I sense around him are dense and are not at all like the personality I see shining through his eyes.

He starts to cry. His tears are of relief, cleansing and hope.

I ask Daniel if he's going to be okay now. I hand him a list of phone numbers and tell him to call them immediately if he has other thoughts of suicide.

We hug.

As I turn to leave, I feel the energies in the room lighten. Daniel smiles a great big smile, and he takes in a great big new breath. My job here is done. As I walk past the police officers, they stare at me, not sure what to think. I smile, say nothing and walk past them to the van.

We're off to wait for the next call. Hopefully, we'll get to eat some lunch first.

Not all attempted-suicide calls are this easy. Daniel was sensitive, but he'd been overwhelmed with the energies around him and didn't know how to clear out his field. This happens to many of us. We feel our energy levels falling but do nothing about it. A quick shake-off provides a nice pick-me-up and boosts energy levels a few notches. Smudging with sage is also very beneficial. However, when burning sage, make sure it's completely out before storing it away. Sage has a tendency to smolder and can restart if one isn't careful.

Here in the Phoenix area, sage grows wild. If you plan to harvest sage, there are a few guidelines to follow for optimum results. Always leave an offering to the Earth when you take sage. This can be in the form of a small pinch of tobacco, birdseed, or water for the plants around where you harvest the sage. This is a gentle way to give back to the Earth. Never harvest sage from the side of a busy roadway. Automotive fumes are absorbed into the plant, and such plants are not pure enough for use in a smudging ritual.

Once a few branches of sage have been collected, either tie them into a small bundle for burning, or burn just a few leaves at a time. Light the sage on fire and allow it to burn for a minute. Then blow out the flame and fan the sage. Smoke will billow with an aromatic smell. Fanning the sage or a slow, steady puff of air will keep the sage burning and smoking. Let it fill the room. Go to the four corners of each room, allowing the smoke to drift to each corner. Sage smoke is believed to remove all negative energies.

There are other ways to clear out an aura that are less smoky. Soaking in a bathtub with some great aromatherapy oils can clear the negative energies from one's field also. Adding a drop of food coloring to the water to create a favorite color also will assist in relaxing the body, mind and spirit.

As relaxation begins to creep into your body and mind, energies aligned with your highest good can start to rebuild and replenish. By doing this, new and clearer energies can push the negative ones out of the body. Allow your body to relax in the warm water, and breathe in the aromatherapy oils. As you relax, see the color you chose for your bathwater begin to flow into the cells of your body. As this imagery continues, relaxation replaces stress and tension within your body. You will then allow tension and stress to flow out of your body into the water. When you get out of the bathtub and the water starts flowing down the drain, imagine all the stress and tension flowing with it, out of your house and out of your life.

Not everyone has time for a leisurely bath every day, so a nice salt scrub in the shower also works wonders. I prefer sea salt, available in local grocery stores, for this activity. After my normal shower, I pour a bit of sea salt into my hand and start rubbing it into my skin. A gentle, circular motion works best. Make sure you have no open wounds, because salt will cause a burning sensation.

Sea salt is also a great exfoliate for dry skin, and it's very inexpensive. To make bath salts, pour sea salt into a container, add a drop or two of a favorite fragrance, and close the container for a few hours. On reopening the container, it will take on the characteristics of your chosen scent, and be ready to use. I like to add a few drops of fresh-squeezed citrus juice and a bit of citrus zest because I have so many citrus trees in the backyard and hate to see them go to waste. Just know that fresh fruit juice needs to be used within a few days. Other aromatherapy oils, when added to salt, will stay fresh for weeks.

Another easy way to clear your energy field is to "tone." Toning is just a long, repeated note made by your own voice. It doesn't matter if you have good pitch or no pitch at all. As you choose a note, let it be long and strong. See the negative energies being released from your body. With each added tone, see positive energies coming into your body.

My husband prefers the sage to my toning. Most of my family members have the sound of "Lee" somewhere in their names. On one rare occasion, we were all gathered together, joyously singing "Happy Birthday" at the top of our lungs. My husband instantly surmised that we all sang in the key of "Lee"!

Not necessarily a compliment, but we do sing with gusto!

8
Night Shift

My next shift is a night shift. It begins at 8 p.m. and ends at 8 the next morning. Some nightshifts are routine, but others become a string of never-ending dashes from one point to the next. This was going to be one of those nights.

We finish our pre-service checklist and make ourselves available for calls when the tones go off. It's a 963: a car accident involving a fatality. We hurry into the van, check our maps, and alert the Alarm Room that we're off and running.

As we drive up to the scene, police vehicles and fire apparatus line the streets. Crime tape stretches around the yard, where a large crowd gathers. This will not be a short, easy call.

We park two blocks away and go in search of the command unit. As we walk, energy generated by the crowd bristles with a heavy agitation. The hair on my arms stands at attention. Auras of people are quickly deepening to dark red. I sense wonder and grief mixed with the emotions this night. We walk a bit faster to find the commander in charge.

The commander is very happy that we've arrived, almost too happy. He tells us that things could get ugly really fast out here tonight. He warns us to stay on guard and to stay together or near an officer. Rarely are we warned to such a degree.

What could be happening?

The commander explains that a young teenage boy stole the keys to a family member's vehicle and crashed it into a neighbor's giant palm tree. If you're not familiar with palm trees, they're a solid, immovable force offering no flexibility whatsoever at the base. Hitting a large palm tree full force and without brakes is like hitting a hundred-year-old oak tree or a reinforced cement pillar.

We walk to the accident scene just in time to hear one of the Fire Department paramedics pronounce the kid dead. The family is unaware of this outcome, and notification falls to me, the "green shirt" of the team.

All this was so avoidable. Had the boy only worn a seatbelt, he would still be alive.

I use a wide, sweeping glance to check out the crowd in order to find the immediate family. The most prominent grief comes from a small group about thirty feet away. I make my way over to them, weaving through the crowd with my partner trailing closely behind. As we near the targeted area, I feel a chill in the warm night air. I know what this means, so I prepare myself. In the crowd stand the mother, a few brothers and cousins, and a close friend of the deceased boy.

"Hello. My name is Sherri and I'm with the Phoenix Fire Department. The paramedics did everything they could to save your loved one, but I'm sorry to inform you that your son has died."

All hell breaks loose when I deliver these words. It was as if I'd yelled "fire!" in a crowded theater.

The family rushes past me to get to the boy, but police are there to stop them. True, it's a crime scene and no one is allowed to tamper with evidence, but the family is also being restrained because of the massive amount of head and facial injuries the kid received from the force of impact. No one should have to see a loved one looking like that.

I talk to the family, but they don't listen. Surrounding hues become darker as their anger intensifies. We're sitting on a time bomb. I take a few steps away as the police try to restore order.

Again I feel the cool air. I need cold water to clear my head of the crowds and their angry thoughts, so I move back to the van. The chill follows me. When I reach the van, I decide to ask who this is. I ask who needs my attention, and then I listen. I hope whoever it is has a better solution for handling this tense situation.

The boy makes contact, and he's confused. He wants to know what's happening to him and why everyone is so upset. "Wow,"

I think. He has no idea what just happened to him. How do I to tell him that he just died on account of a stupid, irreversible mistake?

This is the second time I have to deliver my speech to a dead person. I tell him who I am, and I let him know that he was in a car crash and didn't make it: as in dead. He tells me he can't possibly be dead because he's talking to me. I inform him that I hear him, but that no one else here does.

His energy pulls away, leaving momentarily, then returns. Now he wants to know why no one can hear him but me. Again, I explain that he's dead. He booms a huge burst of energy at me, followed by a string of curse words. Then he's gone again.

I definitely need cool water now. A spirit has never "cussed me out" before! I tell myself, "I love my job, I love my job…" as I splash icy water on my face and neck.

I scan the crowds to relocate the mother. She wants to see her baby. Over and over she repeats, "Please, just let me see my baby." I tell her I'll check with the police and be right back.

I approach the vehicle and hail the officers investigating the crash. I ask if the mother can see the scene to verify it's her son. The officers tell me to take a look for myself and to use my own judgment. I glance inside. It's not a scene I would like to see if it were my loved one, so I head back to the mother.

A few steps away from the crash, the coolness revisits. The young man is still confused. He says he can't get back into his body and he doesn't want to be dead. I explain that there isn't a thing anyone can to do at this point. He must accept his fate and move on to the light and love which will soon beckon. This isn't going over well for him, and he vanishes again without warning.

I approach the family to confirm that the victim is indeed the son, and I recommend to the mother that she not look at the body. I explain that she really doesn't want her last memory to be of him in that condition. I sit her down on the ground and hold her as she sobs into my shoulder. The chill whips around me again, and I know that the son is close. He wants me to tell his mom that he's sorry, that he never meant for any of this to happen. He wanted to go see his girlfriend and show off the sleek, new vehicle. As he rounded the corner and stepped on the gas, the car moved so fast that he lost control.

His mother stops crying for a minute and looks around as if she senses her son nearby. He is so sorry that he has caused so much pain to his mother. I try to comfort her, but as more family members arrive, grief levels escalate. In the distance, there's a commotion, and police run in that direction. Bitter and angry younger male relatives are trying to force their way past the police line.

The young man wants no more bloodshed. He seems more accepting of his circumstances, and I ask him what I can do to calm everyone down. He tells me to call the family priest; that this man has a way with the family and has settled arguments before. I confirm the parish name with his mother and step away to make the call.

No one answers at the church, so I do the next best thing. I arrange for the Fire Department's chaplain to come on scene until their family priest is located. The Fire Department has priests and minsters on call to assist when we need them, and boy did I need them!

Once the chaplain arrives, auras lighten and change to less intense colors. Moods calm down as the young men release part of their anger into the night. The deceased wants to be sure he's going to be okay in the next life, and he requests last rites. I ask the mother if she would feel better if the priest performs this ritual. She says it would help her more than we could possibly know. The priest agrees, even though the young man has already passed away.

We all watch as the priest makes his way over to the vehicle to perform the last rites. As he finishes, the coolness returns once again. I ask the young man what he wants this time. He says he feels a strange pulling, but he doesn't want to leave just yet. He wants his mother to know how much he loves her and how sorry he is for this tragic ending. I assure him I'll let her know, but that it's time for him to let go. He flashes a sweet smile, and reaches out to touch his mother's face one last time. She closes her eyes and makes the sign of the cross. He turns away. I feel him no more that evening.

I sit with the mother for some time afterward, holding her hand and handing her tissues. I reassure her that her son loves her very much and that he'll always be in her heart if she ever wants to talk to him. The priest from the family's church finally arrives and takes them all inside the home to grieve in private. We gather our notes for the reports and the endless paperwork, and we make for the van.

The rest of the night is filled with indifferent calls. We don't make it back to the station until the sun sends out its glorious rays. I roll up my sleeping bag, clean up my bunk area, and say goodbye to the crew.

It's time to go home to get some real sleep.

9
Learning Boundaries

No, the sky isn't the limit

Sometimes, on my drives home from the station, I know I'm not the only on in the car. That was bothersome until I declared ground rules. I now have a steadfast rule that clearly states: NO BOTHERING ME WHILE I'M DRIVING.

Sudden, unexpected appearances in my rearview mirror of a soul popping up in the back seat would cause anyone to spin into a screeching driving mishap. I'm not sure a police officer would go for the story that a dead person distracted me momentarily, thereby causing the accident.

"Honest, officer. It wasn't my fault!"

That would really fly in court.

I have another rule: NO BOTHERING ME IN MY BATHROOMS. That's my private time and is definitely not a time I like to share with others.

When I realized I had these gifts, I would get very excited, and I wanted to talk to any guide or soul who would take the time. But establishing borders and limiting the time I spent with them wasn't something explained in any "guidebook."

When I was a child, bathrooms were their favorite places to contact me. There were no external noises such as television or radio, no one in there was already talking with me, and there were no distractions. What a perfect time for souls who want to "reach out and touch somebody." It was fun at first, but over time I was bombarded. I became a basket case about going into bathrooms because I just knew someone would be in there waiting for me.

Eventually, I learned from Anna May, my metaphysical teacher, that I could and should set boundaries and had every right to enforce them. So my new rules were no cars and no bathrooms. I wasn't specific enough the first time I did this and only specified my bathroom. Well, needless to say, one doesn't always use one's own bathroom during the course of the day.

There they would be, all lined up, waiting for me in a public bathroom, a friend's bathroom or even my own guest bathroom. I learned to be very specific when stating wishes and intentions from that point on.

These boundaries work on a variety of levels, including for my furry friends at home. My pets follow me everywhere I go in the house, leaving no doubt what room I'm in, should my husband need to look for me. As I walk from room to room, the head of the parade, my husband, Yale, will comment, "Mom's on the move. Strike up the band!"

Cats don't like spirits, so when I stated my rules about NO BATHROOMS, the spirits left, and the cats were in. Before, when spirits were allowed, the cats followed me to the bathroom door and stopped short, staring into the room as if they were looking at or for something. Not one of the cats would come in with me.

Now, with rules in place, we all pile in as though it's some giant safety zone.

I think pets see and sense much more than we do. My cats like to stare past a person as if they're reading the aura or seeing who's spiritually hanging out with them. When I teach meditation classes in my home, my cats come down to the 'meditation pit' to claim their spots, waiting patiently for students to arrive. They have a favorite student, Paul, whom they like to freak out at every opportunity. Paul takes his customary spot near the steps. The cats stare just past him, or a few feet above him, for minutes on end. They move their heads as if watching something or someone move around Paul: concentration at it most focused levels. This has tendency to unnerve even the strongest of students, like his wife, Linda.

Setting boundaries is a very simple thing to do, as long as wants and demands are specific. As stated, "they" aren't allowed to contact me in any car that I'm driving unless it's a lifesaving emergency. Then, and only then, will their interference be tolerated. I've also made clear that any bathroom is off limits unless I request their presence. Another request is that I don't want to see them during the night near my bed, in my house, or when I least expect them. I request a warning signal such as that cool-air feeling or a smell that I specify beforehand.

I don't like surprises that could take years off my life!

I also don't like "things that go bump in the night." Horror films aren't my favorite genre. Deep down, I'm a total chicken: It's as simple as that! I don't wish to be awakened in the middle of the night, like the lady in the TV show *Medium*, only to see dead people around our bed. I'm also very sure that my husband doesn't want to be jolted out of slumber by my hysterical screaming!

Set boundaries and be firm about them. Changing boundaries is easily done by adding or subtracting to suit the situation.

As a child, I saw "things" in the dark. I was so afraid of the dark that my younger brother, Bob, would tease me by turning off the hall light, leaving me in the torturous darkness of my room. He didn't understand that I was never alone in my room. There was always someone in there with me. My mother said I had an overactive imagination, but she would turn the hall light back on to appease me. A few minutes later, brother Bob would sneak attack again just to hear my terrified voice: "Turn on the hall light!" I would repeat it like a *mantra*, eyes squeezed tightly shut, curled up under the blankets, waiting for one of my parents to turn the light back on and rescue me from the dark.

The spirits never seemed to bother me much when the lights were on or when daylight streamed into my room. They came only after dusk, when shadows engulfed everything. I could see them move in the dark. It seems that I have always sensed them, but I didn't want to see them.

In the daylight, they would read to me and tell me stories of lifetimes long ago. I played in my room all by myself for hours on end. But once darkness fell, the room took on a discomforting dimension.

Not only was my room odd, but things just outside were scary too. Outside my second-story bedroom window was a huge and ancient elm tree. I often told my mother that one day that tree was going to come crashing into my room. She reassured me the tree was very healthy, and that my room and I would be quite safe. Just in case, I asked my spirit friends to keep me safe from that tree, because I knew differently. A few days after we moved from that house, a freak summer storm blew through town, and the tree crashed into the house, taking out most of my old room!

As a child growing up in a small town in the Midwest, my strange stories and unnatural antics, as they were labeled, were attributed to an overactive imagination. I had imaginary friends, but I never thought they were real like me, so I rarely mentioned them to anyone, for fear of ridicule. I kept to myself, choosing one or two school chums as close friends. I played with everyone while at school, but once that bell rang, I went home to my room to be with my "special" friends.

I was routinely invited to go to friends' homes to play or for sleepovers, but rarely did I invite anyone over to my house. The possibility of them overhearing me with my imaginary playmates was too much of a risk. I didn't want them to think I was weird, let alone be exposed to public ridicule.

Going to a new friend's house was an adventure in itself because their houses had souls in them too, but the families never communicated with their spiritual guests. I never communicated with them either, but they were definitely present. Oddly, no one sensed them but me. I think that by the time I was eight or nine years old, I knew I was very different from all the other kids.

For example, when neighborhood children were choosing sides for the game "Red Rover, Red Rover," I always knew whose name would be called before anyone opened his or her mouth.

My childhood was odd, but still enjoyable. I held great conversations with my pets, and I never really missed the companionship of other children.

During my teen years, I could listen to music and tell you what was going through the artists' minds as they wrote and recorded a particular piece, explanations later verified through radio and television celebrity interviews. I spent many years in my room listening to records on my small phonograph, seeing and feeling what the music meant to those who created it.

Teenage years aren't easy for anyone, so you can imagine navigating through mine. Most people's intuitive abilities shut down by this age. I didn't know I could block it off, so mine just kept growing. I tried drugs in high school, but that only heightened experiences I was trying to avoid.

One day, while hanging round the student break area, a few friends came up to chat. One of them looked very out of focus. I thought I needed new glasses, but everyone around her looked just fine. When I looked back at Diane, she was still out of focus. I chalked it up to being a drug flashback.

We all giggled until it was time to go to class, and I didn't see Diane for the rest of the day. The following morning at school, I found out that Diane had been hit by a car the night before and had died!

That shook my soul. If I had known that being out of focus meant you were going to die, maybe I could have said something and saved her. I felt guilty for years for not knowing and not warning her.

A few months after Diane passed away, I happened to meet up with another friend, Darcie, during summer break. She looked out of focus, so I tried to tell her something was wrong. I warned her that she needed to be careful and not to take any chances for the next few days. She just smiled and told me to stay away from the bad drugs.

Darcie and I were to meet up again the following day. The plan was for me to ride my bicycle to her house for lunch. As I started to leave our driveway on my bike, *both* tires went flat! I phoned Darcie to let her know my problem and that I would meet her the following day, after I got my bike fixed. We made the same plans to have lunch and hang out. I reminded her to be very careful. She promised she was going to stay home all day and just hang loose.

That evening on the news, it was announced that Darcie had been shot to death by a cranky neighbor who thought she was playing her music too loudly. Another death I couldn't prevent!

"What good is this stupid gift, if I can't stop these tragic outcomes!" I thought.

I decided that I no longer wanted these gifts, and I turned to alcohol. Drinking numbed my senses -- all six of them. For months I drank whatever alcohol I could get my hands on. My parents were at a total loss to explain my sudden change in behavior. I was at a loss because I couldn't explain to them, let alone myself, why I was self-destructing in plain view.

My downward spiral stretched into several years. During that time, I married and had two children. The marriage ended suddenly when my husband went to work one day and never returned. It took a few weeks to track him down. He'd found a new girlfriend and claimed he was a single guy. At age 22, I found myself with two small babies and a failed marriage. What more could happen to me?

Have you ever heard the saying, "You can run, but you can't hide"?

I'm proof that you can't deny individual purpose and talents. Regardless of how hard I tried, those gifts were always right there, always in the way, always reminding me, always making life way more complicated than it needed to be.

Later, when that out-of-control driver rear-ended me, totaled my car, and sent me into physical therapy, chiropractic sessions and eventually to massage therapy, it was a fateful wake-up call. Forceful things happened on the outside to propel me to look inside. My massage-school instructors became life guides, carefully showing me how to gently and responsibly deal with who I was and what "this package" was all about.

Cheri and Kasha introduced me to focusing, understanding, accepting and nurturing my abilities, not running from them.

I'm ever grateful for my teachers' and Anna May's wisdom. It brought me closer to where I'm supposed to be in my life!

10
Angels and Working Girls

I'm all snuggled down in my cozy firehouse bunk, when room lights flash with a vengeance and a horrific noise pierces the air. Haltingly, I force myself out of a thick grog, not knowing at first where I am, and then realizing I'm on a night shift.

I'm being toned out to a call.

Like a robotic toy, my body swings into a sitting position, feet over the edge of the bed. I reach for my boots. This usually works better if you're awake and have your eyes open. Nevertheless, I locate them, pull them on, grab my coat, and head out of the sleeping quarter into the cold, dark bay where all the emergency vehicles are parked. I accidentally bang into the side of one of the fire engines, and have to sidestep a ladder truck in order to speed my arrival at the crisis response van.

Graceful under fire I'm not.

I open the van door, push the computer button to let the Alarm Room know we're taking the call, run back into the station to use the bathroom, and take a quick glance to make sure I don't look like a wreck. I don't want to be mistaken for part of the emergency scene.

I meet my EMT in the van, and we're off. All this takes less than two minutes. It's a brutal way to wake up, but firefighters spend their lives doing this, being savagely interrupted on every night shift they ever pull.

It's 2 a.m. Nothing good happens on a call at 2 a.m., and this one will be no different. A young mother has awakened to find her newborn cold and unresponsive. She calls 911, and we're sent to assist the paramedics on the engine.

As we approach the small but well-kept house, the captain comes out to meet with us. He lets us know this looks to be a sudden infant death syndrome (SIDS) situation. Baby was fine when the parents laid her down, but when she didn't wake up for her usual feeding, the parents checked on her. Her body was cold to the touch and her tiny chest lay motionless. They attempted CPR, following every detail of the instructions from the 911 dispatcher, but got no results.

The engine was on scene in less then four minutes, but they knew the baby had been gone far too long to try to resuscitate. Calls involving children are always, always hard calls, but newborns who die so suddenly are especially tormenting.

The parents speak very little English, and my Spanish isn't much better. We try to communicate, but nothing in any language can ease their all-consuming anguish.

We hand the parents Spanish-language grief brochures from the van. I hold the mother in my arms while she cries into my green shirt. Comfort is the only thing I can offer. I give her tissues. She cries more. Police detectives will not let the parents hold their baby until their investigation is finished. It seems like an eternity.

Finally, the detectives finish, and they deliver the cold body to the mother's arms. That moment is so excruciating, even the most jaded of hearts can't escape the suffering. I can barely see as I step outside to wipe away tears. Police officers and firefighters do the same. I take a deep breath and walk back inside.

The mother doesn't have a picture of her baby, and she asks if we can take one so she will always remember her daughter's angelic beauty. This request freaks out the detectives because how are they going explain this back at the finishing lab?

I quietly whisper, "Do it."

I swaddle the baby and hand her to her parents as they pose for this surreal family portrait. Tears streak down their disaster-stricken but smiling faces. I step back outside to dry my own tears once again.

Their baby is in good hands. Family love from the "other side" flows easily around and through each member of this family and their home. The baby is far too young to talk to me, but she knows she has fulfilled her promise and purpose. She will watch over her parents and return at a better time for all of them. I tell her I understand why she has to go back, and I thank her for the lessons she has taught all of us this night. I tell her to go to the light when she's ready. Even she hesitates to leave the captivating security and warmth of this family's pure affection.

We stay with the parents until the medical examiner's (ME) staff come to take the baby. The gurney looks the size of the Sahara Desert when the tiny infant is placed on it. The mother returns to desperate crying. ME personnel decide they will carry the baby to their waiting van instead.

As they walk away, one with the baby cradled in his arms, the mother falls to the ground, overwhelmed with despair. I sit on the ground with her and hold her, gently rocking her back and forth, back and forth.

The department arranges for a Spanish-speaking priest to stay with the family. He will be able to start the parents on their path toward healing. We say our goodbyes and climb back into the van. Neither of us feels like going back to sleep, so we drive around aimlessly, telling bad jokes, emergency personnel's way of de-stressing from a hard call. The morning sun breaks through, casting the city in a friendlier look once again.

We don't have to wait long before the next call. It's another code.

It's almost 6 a.m., when, statistically, most codes occur or are discovered. Someone has awakened to find that their loved one has passed away during the night.

The hotel we arrive at has seen better days, and the clientele aren't exactly elite. The captain comes over to brief us.

"Seems there was a party going on in here last night."

He motions for us to follow, and we dutifully fall in behind him. As we turn the side corner of the hotel, we see the police standing around with silly grins on their faces. This is going to be "one of those calls." They can be described as factual scenes or situations in which circumstances provide the true inspiration for urban legends told around campfires. After all, things like that only happen in the movies, right?

A "lady of the evening" explains that she was picking up a few bucks to pay bills because this was the only quick way to get the cash she needed. She said she met up with her "friend," and they came to the hotel. After drinking, smoking various drugs, and just all-out partying, they finally got around to why they were at a hotel. During the act of pleasure, he had a heart attack and died on top of her.

Obviously, she realizes this isn't a good day at the office, but she's far more frightened than she should be. Something doesn't feel right. Per the police, the death of her "friend" appears to be from natural causes, so it wasn't her fault. The couple had already done all the drugs, so she wasn't being "busted" for possession. There's no law against sharing a hotel room so, legally, she's in the clear.

But something is clearly wrong.

I tune into her energies, but she's so closed off I can't reach her. I push on her energy field, and abject fear pushes back. If I'm to make any progress on this call, I have to find the source of her gridlock.

Early mornings during the winter in Phoenix can be chilly, so I ask her if she wants to sit inside our van to warm up. She agrees, and we walk over to the van. I start the motor, and we're soon toasty. I reach for my clipboard and start noting her personal information and responses for my report.

"Nancy" is a possible real first name, but "Smith" doesn't ring true as her last. She doesn't make eye contact and stares at the floor. Every few minutes she looks at her watch, returning her frozen gaze to the van's floor mat, but with increasing tension. I ask Nancy a few more questions. She claims no address, phone number, or social security number. She's petite, looks clean, has nice hair and teeth, manicured nails, and nice clothes. Nancy isn't homeless.

We chat about the weather, cute police officers, and do general small talk. Her energy opens up, and I slowly move forward in my questioning. We get around to men, more specifically, husbands. She tells me her marriage isn't working out well, and that I wouldn't understand. As I share history of my own unfortunate first marriage, she relaxes. I tell her we all make mistakes and that sometimes just getting it out by telling someone can really make it feel so much better.

Silence.

Her frazzled energy moves toward me, warily searching for a sympathetic soul. I gently pat her hand. More silence. Her inner struggle pleads for a way to get whatever is bothering her OUT. I send my energy to surround her like a warm wooly blanket, reassuring her that she will be fine.

Nancy takes a deep breath and begins her story. Her husband walked out on her several weeks before, and she's been trying to patch things up. He complained she didn't earn enough money to support him and the family in the style he felt he deserved. Her day job cut back her hours, so making ends meet for herself and two children was impossible. She decided that prostitution was the only way to get her hands on fast cash.

As she talks, I see the pictures in her mind as vividly as she does. I hand her tissues as she needs them. She worries because she has to go to her husband's apartment to get their kids, then take them to the babysitter's house so she can go to work today. I wonder why the husband can't watch them, since he apparently doesn't hold a job, but decide not to interrupt. Nancy is on a roll.

She tells me she picked up "Frank" at a local nightclub. They drove to the hotel to party and possibly do some business together. They partied well into the night and early morning, as evidenced by the wine bottles, beer cans, and drug paraphernalia strewn around the room. She says he took Viagra® so he could continue. Everything was fine until he began to sweat. He sweated more, then quite a bit more, and his face turned red. She thought Frank was just really into what they were doing, so she kept up her end of the bargain.

Then Frank let out a huge, groaning gasp and collapsed onto Nancy's ninety-pound frame. She thought he was done and waited for him to move. She waited. And waited. Frank outweighed Nancy by close to 300 pounds, and she couldn't move out from underneath him. She called his name and pounded on his shoulders. He didn't respond. Panic set in.

Nancy was having a hard time breathing, and she knew she needed to get out from under Frank before she passed out. She yelled for help.

People in the next room finally called the hotel manager, who showed up at the door, knocking several times. By that time, Nancy could barely talk. When she tells me about the manager finally opening the door, I can feel her humiliation because of the position she was in.

Embarrassed, Nancy tells me, the manager started to shut the door to give them their privacy when she called out for help again. He finally entered the room and rolled Frank off of her. He checked Frank's pulse. There was none. He called 911. By the time the Fire Department arrived, there was nothing they could do for Frank. Police were dispatched to investigate, and the CRT was called out to calm Nancy.

Nancy finishes her story. I continue sending comforting energy and tell her I'll be right back. I want to find out how much longer she needs to remain on scene. I step out of the van and walk over to the group of officers to find out who's in charge. I tell the charge officer Nancy's new story and ask when she'll be allowed to go home.

As the details come out, the faces of officers within earshot light up with total amusement.

I walk back to the van to tell Nancy the bad news. She'll be detained until an investigator can interview her about the details of the night's events. She's visibly upset. Her bloodshot eyes are rimmed in red from tears and lack of sleep. I give her more tissues and lead her to a police car so she can stay warm.

Frank didn't contact me. True to form, when someone passes away unexpectedly, they're confused and tend to stay very close to their bodies. By the time we arrived, the hotel room had been roped off with crime-scene tape, so we had no access. I would dearly love to have heard his side of the story. It took five grown, in-shape men to lift Frank's flabby, white dead-weight onto the gurney.

My partner and I get back into the van and shake our heads. Even though tonight is a traumatic experience for this woman, protocol tolerates absolutely no disrespectful comments or joking while on scene. We don't make eye contact until we drive about two blocks away. Then we look at each other and burst into laughter.

The scene in *The Wizard of Oz*, when the house lands on one of the witches, leaving only her red and white striped leggings and black pointy shoes sticking out from underneath the house, is Nancy stuck underneath Frank's last hurrah. At last I have my own first-hand urban legend to share with firefighters when they spin their wild tales.

Please understand that we're genuinely saddened when someone dies. But you have to admit, this makes a hell of a story around a campfire on a star-filled night!

Maybe Nancy will take up weight-lifting.

11
The Plot Thickens

There's one group of tones I especially dread, the drowning tones. They hold a very distinctive pitch and sound, and they usually happen during the day when a parent or babysitter slips away for only a moment to answer the phone.

So when we hear them in the middle of the night, I ask myself, "Who drowns at one o'clock in the morning?"

As we drive to the scene, my young partner Jay -- known to me affectionately as "Punk-ass" -- and I conjure up possible scenarios. My guess is there was a wild party, someone dove into the pool and never surfaced. Everyone else was too passed out to notice until now.

Jay leans more toward the gruesome side: Someone finally came home after bar-closing time to discover a body in the pool. Either way, it's not going to be a good call. We both feel it in our water-logged bones.

We're not surprised to see flashing lights from both police and fire vehicles at the scene. We find a spot to park the van, and we start looking for the officer in charge. He finds us instead. This isn't going to be a good morning, and it will be a long one, he tells us. He wants to know if we have any coffee in the van, because we seem to carry just about everything else. We're sad to inform him that we don't have any coffee, but offer what we do have. He declines with a smile.

He walks us away from the crowd of public-service and news-media people so he can tell the story without being overheard.

It seems that an older man and his wife had been celebrating his birthday and decided to spice up their sex lives. While in their backyard hot tub together, someone came up with an idea to try the new craze of "auto-erotica" sex. How and why they decided to do this is fuzzy, the officer explains, but the man is dead and has an object lodged in his throat that prevented him from breathing during the sex act.

Jay and I look at each other. It wakes us up faster than any caffeine. We ask the police officer what he needs from us, and he points to four kids sitting on a curb, huddling close to each other. Police will be questioning the wife for a long while, so someone needs to watch the kids until a relative can take over.

I make my way toward the kids and introduce myself. We take them over to our van and put them inside to keep them warm and away from the television crews. The kids don't know what's happened to their dad or why their mom is in a police car. The oldest of the four children is a young teenager, and he's old enough to understand. It's a matter of time before I have to tell them their dad is dead. I need to do this before they find out on their own.

The teen remembers their grandparents' phone number. I write it down, get out of the van, and wade through crime tape and increasing numbers of reporters and camera crews to get to the officer in charge. He looks at me and the slip of paper as though I were offering him a plate of *Fear Factor* delicacies. He pushes my hand back, saying that I'm the "touchy-feely one" on this scene and that I should make the call. He'll stand by if I need assistance.

I unfold the paper and dial the number. It's now close to 2 a.m., and the phone rings endlessly. Finally a sleepy voice answers. I start off by saying my much-practiced lines: "Hello, my name is Sherri and I'm with the Phoenix Fire Department. There's been an accident involving your son-in-law. Your four grandchildren need you. Can you come to their house right away?"

I have to repeat myself several times before it sinks in. The grandparents let me know they live just a few minutes away. I tell them a squad car is probably outside their door by now, and that officers will escort them safely here.

"We'll be right over."

Click.

As they pull up to their grandchildren's home, the episode is one straight out of the movies. The usually quiet scene is swarming with uniforms, police cars, fire trucks, ambulances and TV cameras. With terrified faces, the couple hurry to our van to hug the children waiting anxiously outside. I introduce my partner and myself, and let them know the kids are fine but that there is another problem. I ask Jay to take the kids back into the van so I can talk to the grandparents alone.

With the children inside, I turn to talk, but the color of their faces vanishes. I follow the direction of their stares to where they see their daughter in the back of the police car, about thirty feet away. They move toward her, but I reach out to stop them. I introduce them to the police officer in charge, and he explains what's going on. He says their son-in-law has died and then quickly looks at me again, hoping I'll take over the conversation.

I reiterate what we know so far, and that I'm sorry to inform them their son-in-law has passed away. This time the words sink in. The grandfather reaches for his wife to support her shock. I give them a few moments, hand them tissues, and let them know I'm here if they have questions about what happens next.

And they do have questions. I don't have all the answers, but assure them more information will be available as time goes by. They join the children inside the van.

The kids ask about their mom and dad. Both grandparents look to me and ask if our team would please explain it to the kids. I accept, knowing the toughest part of this job is explaining death to a child. We do our best, and hope they have a good support system to get them through it. The kids seem to understand when I tell them, but it hurts. They cry and turn to each other. They know this isn't a television show: The aching outcome isn't going to change.

A strained but brave, stiff-upper-lip smile comes over the grandmother's face as she squeezes my hand. I send her a bit of healing *chi* energy. The pain she now faces will take on added dimensions in coming weeks. She continues to hang onto my hand, as if she knows this momentary "*chi* fill-up" will help sustain her later on.

The grandparents decide to take the kids back to their own house, away from all the flashing lights and the crime-scene tape. We walk them to the police car, hand over our famous trauma teddy bears, and wish them the best of luck. They drive off with phone numbers of counselors, hotlines, grief support groups, and books to read to the kids to nurture them through this tragedy. We also give them information for handling their own grief.

Since there isn't much else we can do, we inform the officer in charge, make ourselves available to the Alarm Room, and head back to the station. The rest of the shift is uneventful, but I still wonder. The deceased father was over 100 yards away, so I couldn't pick up his energy, nor could he pick up mine. I never had the chance to help in that way.

Sometimes doing nothing is the hardest of all.

Another strange incident occurs on a day when Carole and I are partnered. No calls are coming through, so we find ourselves driving aimlessly around Phoenix, and we finally decide to visit a few of the city's sixty or so fire stations.

When you want a call, it doesn't come. When you don't need them, they come at you like avalanching snow.

Checking out another fire station is a guaranteed call getter, but we do it anyway. After spending a few minutes saying hello to old friends and meeting a few new ones, we get our wish. Pagers and radios go off, and we both jump.

The call is a 901 (dead body) found on the side of a mountain.

This might be a real call or it might not because hikers can be mistaken in reporting dead bodies. What they see most of the time is discarded clothes, a dead animal, or just twisted branches that look like a body.

Carole and I review the details, trying to determine why we're being sent out. Maybe the hiker is shaken up and just needs a ride back to his car.

We pull up at the base of the mountain and the usual scattering of police cars. One of the homicide detectives, whom we know well, walks up to greet us, asking how we are and wanting to know if we have any of that "cold water" on us. We direct him to the back of the van. As he grabs a cold bottle out of the ice chest, he tells us about the body the hiker found. He says that when he found out we were the team that day, and knowing how much we like to learn new things, he thought he would invite us over.

The detective tells us the victim looks to be a transient or homeless person. It seems the police picked up his girlfriend a few weeks earlier. She kept telling them she thought her boyfriend was dead, but they put her in jail and never located the boyfriend. All was forgotten until a hiker found him about six weeks later on the side of a small mountain in the middle of Phoenix.

Six weeks of our summer heat and sun can do freakish things to a body. The detective says to follow him for a first-hand education in decomposition.

As we trudge up the hill in the peak of July heat, we ask ourselves if this is going to be worth it. We live here and understand the desert, but temperatures are brutal. Finally, the detective stops and points. There, on the ground about thirty yards down a gully, is an American mummy.

The man is lying on his back. His skin is like tanned leather, and his clothes are shredded. It's hard not to notice that he has no face, only a skull. As the rest of the team maneuvers equipment to our location to remove the body, we step out of the way and watch. This time I was actually looking forward to the cool breeze that tells me a spirit wants to pass on a message, but it never comes.

It's over 110 degrees and not even noon.

As specially-trained firefighters and police engineer the recovery and get the body into the body bag, the man's skull detaches from his body rolls down the hill. Everyone stops and stares as it bounces end over end down the slope. I'm the only one not carrying equipment, so the retrieval job falls to me. I make the trek down the mountain to where the skull is resting. Good thing I'm wearing gloves and have a sinus condition.

This is one assignment I hope I never repeat.

Recovery completed, the body part and I climb our way back up to the group. I'm almost there when my mouth takes command of the day. Holding the skull aloft in one hand and sending forth my best Shakespearean voice, "Alas, poor Yorrick, I knew him well!"

Everyone bursts into laughter. It strikes the detective's funny bone so hard that he loses his balance and almost repeats the traveling skull's journey, until the fire captain next to him instinctively grabs for him.

We mean no disrespect to the dead, but sometimes things simply have to lighten up.

The trip down the mountain is uneventful. The detective comes over to the van, declaring that it's a good thing he no longer writes tickets because he could think of a few for me that day. He grins and hugs me, saying that he would remember this one for a long time to come. We distribute cold water and go back into service.

Most days have a theme. Whatever happens first seems to set

the pace for the rest of the shift. Carole and I thought that mountainside call couldn't be topped. We should have known better.

This call starts out as a simple transport. We're to meet police officers to take a mother and her two children from their abusive home and drive them to her mother's house across town. This should be quick and easy.

When we pull up to the residence, the officer is overjoyed, not just happy, to see us. Not a good sign in our line of work. We ask where the mom and kids are, and he says that the mom and one of the kids are sitting over in the shade, while the second child is locked in the caged backseat of his patrol car.

Carole and I look at each other, and then at his car. Sure enough, there's a small boy, about three years old, in the back seat.

We get the mom and the first child comfortably situated in the van and go with the officer to get the remaining child. The officer wishes us the best of luck. He opens the door and takes a giant step backward. We don't heed these warning signs, and are lulled into goo-goo land by the boy's miniature size and darling face.

He explodes out of the car like a tornado. I reach for his hand as he flies by and am rewarded with a debilitating adult-level kick to my shin.

The angelic face, paired with the verbiage spewing from his potty mouth, stops us dead in our tracks. We thought we had heard everything, but that child taught us a few new ones. I don't know how, but we finally corral him into the van. Getting him belted into a child-safety car seat takes both of us, and the detective more time than we care to admit.

On the way across town, we inform the mom that her choice to remain in an abusive relationship is harming her children, and that she needs to consider their welfare, even if she isn't concerned about her own. We give her brochures on domestic violence, lists of agencies that offer assistance, hotline numbers, and a few more words of advice. When we pull up to the front of the grandmother's residence, I let Carole go first to unleash our new little friend from the car seat.

Once his seatbelt is off, the kid bounds out of the van with a vengeance, doing his level best to make a run for it. I grab him and lead him up to his grandma's front door. He fights, kicks and screams the whole way. Mom, clutching her few possessions, is too tired to care. Carole brings up the rear with the other brother, who walks sedately alongside her.

I ring the doorbell. The lady who answers isn't excited about the "return of the prodigal son" – or daughter in this case. Obviously, there's no love lost between mother and daughter. Who knows what caused the rift, but it runs deep.

I say a silent prayer that they can somehow heal it during this time together. The door opens wider, and the kids dash inside. The daughter tells her mom she left her boyfriend and wants to come back home. Mom agrees, and we begin to think that we're all done here.

The teddy bears. We forgot the teddy bears!

We go back to the van to get two bears for the boys. We always try to leave bears with the kids as a positive ending to our calls. But before we can step back into the house, the tiny terrorist comes flying out. Like a matador, I deftly turn sideways, using Carole as my cape. It's her turn to take it in the shins. But she has worked with me too long, and also makes a sidestep, allowing the kid full access to me.

I shriek!

The young boy rushes up to me, grabs the bear, spews out a few more obscenities, and disappears into the house. The other brother thanks us and, as we turn to leave, the door crashes open and the tornado comes roaring back out. He makes a run straight for me, but this time I stand my ground.

He gives me a hug and chirps, "I love you, mother******," then disappears back into the house. Carole and I just stare at the closed door for a moment before she bursts into laughter, and we turn toward the street to leave.

We climb back into the van, glad to be safe, and notify the Alarm Room we're available for another call. Is this going to be the theme for today? Should we pack it up and call it a day? But duty calls and we head back to the station for a nap.

We should have paid attention to our instincts. Carole is just settling into her soap opera when the crisis-care call comes in. We get into the van wondering what could top this day, but we don't say it out loud in case it could actually jinx us. Neither one of us is superstitious, but why rock the boat?

We pull up to a large bus stop at one of the malls and spot our customer quite easily. She's a large woman, possibly in her 70s, wearing a nylon jogging suit complete with lined jacket. It's the middle of the day and temperatures are hovering around 112. No one knows how long she has been there, but it has been at least several hours. She has been sitting in that same spot, rocking back and forth, and holding onto her baby doll and a melted box of candy.

I ask the woman her name, but she doesn't respond. When the fire engine arrives, one of the medics tries to takes her pulse, but she refuses to let any man near her. Carole volunteers to take her vitals while I reassure the woman we're all here to help.

The helmet on the woman's head suggests that she's seizure-prone, so I asked if we can look through her big suitcase to get more information. She nods permission. New, unopened bottles of shampoo, conditioner, toothpaste, toothbrush, deodorant, and an expensive DVD player tell us she isn't homeless. She's clean, wears nice clothes and has an expensive outfit on her doll. Obviously, someone looks after her.

But what happened? Where's her caretaker? Did this woman wander away? Is anyone looking for her?

Police are called in to assist, and we hope someone has filed a missing-person report. The officers check their systems and find no such report. What next? We're at a bureaucratic standstill. The police won't take her because she hasn't committed a crime. Fire personnel can't take her because her vital signs are good and she doesn't need medical attention. CRT can't take her because there's nowhere to take her. Shelters require a name and a social security number before admittance, and we have no information to give them.

So there we all sit, three police officers, four firefighters, my partner and I, and a large crowd of onlookers. Lots of suggestions come from all directions, but no solutions.

The lady is getting very hot in the afternoon sun, so I gently remove her helmet. I ask her to take off her jacket, but she refuses as long as the men are close by. We ask the guys to step back. I kneel down to make eye contact. I wrap invisible love and energy from my heart around her. She grabs my hand and doesn't let go.

We finally convince our Jane Doe to remove her jacket. Once off, we see that her skin is extremely overheated. Her face is getting redder, and she's sweating more than she should. That gives us our temporary answer. Why don't we transport her to the hospital for heat exhaustion?

The captain on the fire engine agrees, and arranges for a rescue unit to come and transport her to a hospital.

While we wait for the rescue operation, we try every which way to Sunday to get her to tell us her name and where she comes from. Labels on her medication bottles in her bag have been peeled off. No name, no access to pharmacy identification records, nothing.

When the ambulance arrives, we're confronted with a new problem. The crew consists of two men. Our Jane Doe refuses to go with them under any circumstances. Her grasp on my hand turns into a death grip, so it's decided that I'll accompany her to the hospital.

Once there, we try to say our good-byes, but she still won't let go of my hand. When I do get free, she starts wailing, rocking and causing quite a commotion in the ER. Either Carole or I have to stay with her. The nursing staff is just too busy to devote that kind of attention to anyone not on emergency status. So we sit with "Jane" and continue to try to get her name or any useful information. We find a sketchpad in her suitcase with beautiful drawings. She nods that she is the artist and drew everything herself. We ask her to write her name, but she just rocks back and forth.

Finally a nurse's aide comes down from one of the floors. They seem to hit it off, so Carole and I sneak away to make calls to arrange some sort of assistance for this woman.

No name and no social security number gets us no help from anyone anywhere. Shelters won't take her, care centers won't take her, adult social services won't take her, and now, at 6 p.m. on a Friday, no one is answering their phones. We're at a loss once again. As our shift ends, we're still at the hospital. Nothing more can be done until Monday, so we concede defeat. Jane Doe will remain at the hospital for awhile.

We say our goodbyes and head out.

Carole and I both call every few hours during the night to see if any information surfaces on our strange friend. It isn't until late the following day that they discover who she is. We're very relieved that Edna, as she turned out to be, really does belong somewhere and that she'll receive better supervision next time.

12
The Call I Recall

Station life is more than just interesting. Most fire stations have about eight firefighters living under one roof at any given time. The engine company has four crew members, as does the ladder truck. Some stations also include a two-member ambulance crew, while others have a battalion chief and his driver, "Haz Mat" (hazardous materials) crews, Department of Public Safety (DPS) people, air-rescue teams, and a variety of other much-needed, specialized crews, including office personnel.

Crews work twenty-four hour shifts, then have forty-eight hours off. There are three shifts, A, B and C. Lighthearted rivalry is rampant among the shift personnel, and firefighters are always making wise cracks about other shifts.

Crews prepare their own meals in the station's kitchen. When not running our own calls, we occasionally share "chow." Some of the best meals I've ever eaten were had around a stainless steel table, eating off hard, beige plastic plates with mismatched silverware, and surrounded by some of the bravest people on earth, listening to their good-hearted stories about work and family.

We CRT types come into their "house" as guests, and if we're very lucky, we become part of their extended family. In most cases, it takes months to earn their respect. We watch them and acknowledge their "firefighter-only" culture. We understand that their connection runs deep. Their lives depend on it.

Volunteers staff the CRT vans twenty-four hours a day, every day. They endure 115-degree days, tromp through monsoon rains, and willingly give up holidays, all so they can earn a fifty cents an hour uniform-clothing allowance. Occasionally, the department receives a grant that makes it possible for selected members to be paid, but money is tight and grants are infrequent. CR supervisors work hard to keep at least two vans up and running at all times.

It's not an easy job.

Since joining the Fire Department, I've been assigned to several different stations, which means earning that respect all over again.

Many of the EMTs who volunteer on CRT vans are firefighter hopefuls, although I'm not one of them. Age and common sense have had to override my occasional visions of grandeur more than once. My abilities lie elsewhere, not to mention the fact that I have grandchildren. My two grandsons, Bradley and Calvin, think I'm the "coolest grandma" because they get to ride in fire trucks and police cars when they come to visit.

Competing in a strenuous fitness test with people half my age isn't a gauntlet I could take up and win. I truly admire everyone who tries to qualify for the Fire Academy, whether they pass or fail. Each testing season, they give it their all, just for a chance to be considered one of the best.

God bless them.

Volunteers on the BHS "green shirt" side of the van have a different reason for being there. As I mentioned earlier, most of them are earning degrees in various areas of counseling or social work. Experience on the vans often meets requirements for the one-on-one counseling time necessary to graduate.

Then there are volunteers like me, who are there to fill a personal need. I'm qualified to do either side of the van, but I think I'm partial to the "green-shirt" side, the warm and fuzzy part of the team, versus the medical side. Each person comes with baggage and a personal reason for volunteering, but most are in a give-back as pay-back mode. The memories of those we help stay with us for life.

One story will stay with me for a very long time, because it was on that day that the tables were turned.

It was a shift much like any other when we got the call. Late morning or early afternoon "code" calls are extremely unusual.

Most people die or are found dead either late at night or very early in the morning.

It's lunchtime, and we're about to sit down at the table with the firefighters when the tones go off. All conversations stop to hear who has to go. Just my luck – it's the CRT van's turn. Jay is especially "bummed" about missing lunch. That skinny boy can pack away more carbohydrates than any firefighter on record, so teasing him about feeding his tapeworm every hour or two is a favorite firehouse pastime.

Lunch will have to wait.

A young teenage boy has died at home. A chill runs up my spine: rough waters ahead.

Jay and I ride in silence as we wind our way through heavy, midday city traffic. We arrive on scene and struggle to find parking. Cars are bumper-to- bumper everywhere, but we find a spot and hike to the house.

Before leaving the van, I reach for an assortment of pamphlets, then pause. I'm not sure why I hesitate, but I know I have to. My feet anchor to a spot and don't move until my mind rehearses different versions about what to tell the parents. I take a deep breath, grab Jay, and head toward the family's front door.

Jay is in the lead, but being the gentleman he is, he opens the large wooden door, allowing me to enter first. Once inside, I hear the father gasp. He stares at me with every bit of his soul. It startles me. I stop so short and fast that Jay walks right into my back. I can't break eye contact! This is no blank stare: It's fully engaged. I assume that the man is so grief stricken that seeing a uniform walk into his house causes reality to come crashing down.

I approach the father and offer my condolences. His eyes grip my every move. He says nothing and gazes, eyes not blinking, mouth gaping like a fish out of water. He looks like he sees a ghost.

Tears well up in his eyes. I steer him over to his couch, and we both sit down. Again, he stares. Finally, I hear soft, jumbled words. I ask him to repeat his statement. Slowly and clearly he says, "Are you the angel God is sending?"

How odd! He was looking into my soul "through rose-colored glasses." As a child, my grandmother often called me an "imp." My character was definitely more that of a mischievous cherub. I'm sure that isn't what the man means.

I assure him that I'm not an angel sent to him by God. He immediately counters by assuring me he knows I'm exactly that. I try to gauge his degree of anguish, thinking this is a new reaction to shock, but the house is too full of all kinds of emotions to get a proper read. I introduce myself to other family members gathering in the room, and I collect the background information.

As I walk back over to the father, he asks if he can speak with me in private. I agree, and we make our way to a spare room. Jay posts himself outside the door and waits. The father sits down in a chair and then nervously, almost excitedly, stands back up again.

He begins his speech by telling me that his name is Armando and that the young boy who passed away is his son. Moments before I walked through the door, Armando says he asked God to send him an angel to give his son a message. Armando tells me that he cried and prayed from his heart. When he was done with his prayer, he said he felt a protective calm. He knew God would answer his prayer. He says he caught a glimpse of his assigned angel and that she had blue eyes.

I'm the only one in the crowded house with blue eyes.

Armando squeezes my arm and pleads with me to share the messages with his son. I try to tell this grieving father that I can't give messages while I'm working. He smiles an infectious smile through his tears and says that it means more to him than I can understand, so I agree.

I take a deep breath, close my eyes, and try to relax. A coolness settles around me, immediately and shockingly followed by a sharp pain exploding in my head! I reach for my temples and grimace.

Armando becomes much more excited and moves closer. He asks me not to think him "strange" when he says he knows I can talk to his son's soul.

I think to myself, "If this man only knew what I do and what I've been through on this job, he'd know that *I'm* the weird one, not him!"

He rambles on that I'm the answer to his prayers, and that he knew I would appear in his home before I ever walked through the door. Now Armando is spooking me out. Being unexpectedly exposed by someone in the outside world is uncomfortable.

I don't want to disappoint him, but no message is coming through from his son. Usually, I have to be very close to the deceased's body before anything can happen. Armando grabs my arm and pulls me towards the door. He is in such a rush, he barges into Jay, who's still standing guard. We scurry to another bedroom, crowded with family members. Jay is a step behind. Armando rattles off something in Spanish, and the crowd parts like the Red Sea before Moses. The boy is lying in peace. I stand quietly for a moment, waiting.

Once I make the connection, messages come like torrential rains. The young boy has so much to say, he tells me, in so little time. I assure him I'll listen and relay everything. I follow the father back into the spare bedroom. Jay positions himself outside the door once more.

Armando and I sit quietly. He takes my hands in his and closes his eyes. He grieves as his son, Mando, tells me that his father isn't to be blamed for not being home when Mando took ill. Mando says it happened very suddenly. One minute he was playing with his younger brother, and the next minute he was in excruciating pain. He shows me his head, the color red gushing outwards.

Mando died from a brain aneurism that wasn't detectable during a normal visit to the doctor's office. He asks that I relay specific messages to his father so the whole family can move on. I agree to act as the "middle man" and relay everything aloud.

With each message, Armando nods in agreement, his eyes so filled with tears that he can't see. He cries without sound in order not to miss a phrase. Mando has explicit comments and prayers for his little brother, who was there when it happened. He goes through a list for other family members and close friends. Armando affirms that no one would know these things except his son.

The series of messages seems to let Armando begin his healing process. He hugs me and tells me to keep him in my prayers until the next time we meet. I thank him and give grief pamphlets and other resources for later on. Young Mando's energy is with me as we leave the premises. I let him know I'll assist him in any way I can if he ever needs me.

Jay and I walk back to our van, notify the Alarm Room we're finished with this call, and are ready to take another whenever they need us.

I'm often curious about what happens to the people after we leave on-call scenes, but we rarely ever reconnect. Somehow, this time, I know things will be different.

Months later, I run into Armando in the breakfast-cereal aisle while grocery shopping. The young father approaches me with a huge smile. He lets me know he was able to move on after he knew his son was okay. He thanks me for the messages that day and wants to know if I could possibly receive anything else from young Mando.

Before I can take a breath to respond, unusual images were snapping and crackling into my head. I know they're not mine by the very nature of the items that appear. First, there's a triple-layer, double-chocolate cake with thick chocolate frosting, a ton of chocolate running down the edges, and crushed chocolate chips sprinkled on top. So much chocolate was involved that I could feel my blood sugars rising and cavities rebelling!

I'm not a big chocolate fan, but obviously, Mando was.

No use making sense of these things, so I describe the image. Suddenly, this grown man is laughing, crying and almost dancing. To the casual observer, it would seem that I'm the cause of it. When I add the detail that a single candle is burning on top of this gooey mess, Armando let out a big whoop.

Armando is ecstatic because it's Mando's birthday that very day.

I hear how Mando, too, wanted to reach out to his father. As a truck driver, Armando was gone from home a lot and missed being around his children. When possible, he tells me, he always made special arrangements for his son to travel across country with him, trips that meant the world to both of them.

So Mando decided to get his father's attention mechanically. He somehow slightly altered the electrical system of Armando's truck, not once, but several times for a couple of days. Finally, Armando took his truck to get the "short circuit" fixed.

The mechanic couldn't find a single problem.

I ask Armando how his truck is doing lately. His happiness fades for a moment.

"Good and not so good."

I advise him to just smile the next time it happens to make the problem go away. "The problem isn't a short in the electrical system," I tell him. "It's Mando playing tricks and saying 'hi!'"

Armando and I talk in the middle of the store for quite some time, oblivious to the odd and occasionally annoyed glances of busy shoppers trying to reach around us for their breakfast cereals. But that doesn't matter.

Seldom do I see the results of the work I do. While I'm doing it, people are completely unaware of both the message and the messenger. I'm an invisible link in their healing process.

Armando and Mando are, however, a singularly different case. Armando knew before he saw me that I could do what I do. His faith, combined with Mando's strong bond with his father, makes our bizarre and wondrous relationship possible.

To this day, Armando and I stay in contact. It thrills, humbles and delights me to pass along messages from Mando whenever they come. This one extraordinary happenstance assures me that using my gift really does count in this world.

Of them all, this remains the call closest to my heart.

Final Thoughts

As I compiled the stories in this book and came to the end, I wondered if there were overall messages; even one.

My original intent was to share stories with you that others have found interesting and to present a glimpse of the "other side." However, there was another side present in every story — the messages I received. In a rare case, I shared the message directly, but mostly I only inferred the messages to the living loved ones. In all cases, it seemed redemptive to the living. They seem to be able to grieve sooner and allow the passing of their loved one.

The truth is, I wouldn't be needed to deliver messages if those messages were delivered while each person was alive.

There is so much to say to each person who touches our lives. Take the time today to share love with family and friends. Talk to your loved ones today – now - before it's too late! Even if things are good, you still need to say the words, and our loved ones still need to hear them aloud or see them in writing. If things have been bumpy, just know it isn't easy for anyone to cut through the veils of years of miscommunication. At one point or another, we have all deceived ourselves in order to protect ourselves or console hurt feelings.

In the end, who really cares that you borrowed my favorite blouse and ruined it, or cut me off in traffic, or betrayed my confidence? As the saying goes, "Don't sweat the small stuff… and it's all small stuff."

Say or do something positive to let each person know he/she is important and that you're grateful. Honor them all! Thank them for their involvement in your life, including the dysfunctional people and moments. They made you stronger by forcing you to look at things you didn't want to see.

Perhaps you should know that when I come home after a code call for a senseless killing by a drunk driver, an infant drowning, or a domestic violence scene of rage, those feelings have an impact on me as well. I've learned not to question why such tragedies occur. They simply do.

I also know there's life after life, otherwise I wouldn't be getting those messages. The communication with someone who has passed isn't guaranteed and doesn't happen on demand, if at all, in some cases. Why wait for the uncertainty when you can certainly say "I love you" now before a loved one ultimately passes?

People ask how I deal with this tension day after day. Over time, I've come to accept that it isn't my tragedy to claim. I only live in the moment with the family and the deceased. Then I go home and let my husband know that I love him. I talk to my parents several times a week. My daughter and I are in constant communication, although she is thousands of miles away, as is my son's family.

I share my feelings with family and friends while they're living now on this side of life. I hope not to say that I wish I'd said something good to them. Who knows when the "bell will toll"?

Mostly what I do is listen to what the deceased are thinking. They don't expect or want me to fix their problems. I'm only there to listen and relay the information. I'm the deceased's last connection to this realm, a connection they really wouldn't need if only they communicated more when they were alive.

Consistently, what the deceased say during those final moments has to do with regret about never having told someone how much they actually cared, before it was too late. The older we get, it seems the more complex the baggage we carry becomes, which needlessly complicates this healing process. Even if efforts are rejected, the attempt is paramount. You did your best. The ball is in their court. Move on.

As I approach each door to deliver death notifications to and about family members, I prepare myself by gathering strong, positive energy. I never know which thought, word, glance or gesture will strike the most soothing chord for the family, but I do know this: Regardless of what I do or how I say it, I'm the messenger who may be changing their lives.

I begin my speech: "My name is Sherri. I'm with the Phoenix Fire Department."

Years down the road, they won't recall my face, but they will remember how they felt when I came to the door. For many, at that moment, I'm all they have during the crucial initial hours until their relatives arrive. And so I listen. They cry. I hand them tissues. A minute goes by. More crying. Another minute passes. We've made it through another moment, and perhaps it's a moment closer to healing.

I acknowledge that my gift is rare. I often wrestle with it myself. It's not a talent that I command, but rather one that I respond to. Sometimes I may be able to assist those who want closure after tragedy. If it helps, it helps.

You create your own reality. Own it, and be a friend and a loved one. What else can one do?

The opportunity, choice and responsibility of making these unique differences in the lives of strangers in my community infuse my life with meaning and purpose. It was my parents who taught me the basis of most world religions: "Do unto others as you would have them do unto you."

I like to think I'm following their advice and setting a good example for my two children and three grandchildren. One day, when it's my turn, I hope there's a crisis response team available for my family.

With ease and grace, may your final time be comforting for you as well as for those you leave behind.

Glossary

901 – This is the code for a dead body.

901H – This is the code for a dead body with "foul play" involved, such as murder. The "H" stands for homicide.

918 – This is the code for a mentally unstable person, or one with an altered sense of reality.

961- This is the code for a car accident with no injuries involved.

962 – This is the code for a car accident with injuries involved.

963 – This is the code for a car accident with a death involved.

AIQ - Available In Quarters. Acronym used when the CR Team is at the fire station and tones (signals) for it will sound in the station.

Alarm Room – The "911" center where all emergency calls are handled.

AOI – Available On Incident – Acronym used when the CR Team is finished assisting someone but will stay on scene until needed elsewhere. The Alarm Room will tone the team on their radio and pager.

AOR – Available On Radio. – Acronym used when the CR Team is out in the community and can be reached by radio.

Battalion Chief – the BC is in charge of seven fire stations and their personnel. He or she is the commander or the "go-to guy" at any scene.

BHS – Behavioral Health Specialist. On the CR Team, the BHS provides immediate crisis intervention and/or victim assistance, valuable support, information and referrals to people in crisis. He or she also facilitates communication between the people involved and the fire and police personnel. The BHS works in partnership with an EMT, and maintains professional, accurate records of all calls

Blue Shirt – The blue shirt is worn by the EMT on the CR Team..

Captain – The company officer, in charge of a truck and crew. Most crews consist of a captain and three firefighters. They are considered the backbone of the Fire Department.

Code, Coded – When a person ceases to breathe and his or her heart ceases to beat properly. Some people can be revived after they have coded.
Coroner - A coroner is responsible for investigating deaths, particularly those happening under unusual circumstances.

CR Team – Consists of two members. There must always be at least one BHS. The second member can be either a BHS or an EMT.

CR Van – The fifteen-passenger van contains two crew members, radios, maps, computer and navigation system, first aid supplies, oxygen tanks, Latex gloves, an automatic external defibrillator (AED), blankets, burn out boxes, flares, road safety kit, and safety vests. Vans also carry a filing system containing over fifty different pamphlets dealing with death, grief, SIDS, coping with tragedy, after-the-fire assistance, homeless shelter info, lists of mortuaries, and much more. There also are child car seats, water coolers filled with ice, bottled water and sports drinks, plastic fire helmets, and our famous "trauma teddies," which are distributed to comfort younger clients.

Drop for Chow – Paying money for the meals served on a given day. Everyone at the station pays an agreed-upon amount for meals and snacks.

EMT – Emergency Medical Technician. On the CR Team, he or she provides basic medical assistance to clients as needed. The EMT operates the van, facilitates radio communications, works in partnership with the BHS, and helps maintain van equipment and supplies.

ER – The Emergency Room, located within a hospital, is where sick or injured people go for initial medical treatment.

Green Shirt – This is the BHS on the CR Team. BHSs wear green shirts and are considered the "touchy-feely" members of the team. They have many hours in training to handle the emotional needs of clients.

ME – Medical Examiners are highly trained physicians who make public inquiries into all sudden and unnatural deaths.

On a Call – Term used when the when the CR Team is on the scene of an incident.

Paramedic – An EMT with advanced life-saving skills.

Repeat Flyers – Clients who abuse the "911" system by calling emergency personnel to non-emergencies over and over again.

Rescue Unit – An ambulance.

Responding – Term used when the CR Team is on the way to an incident.

Shift – For a CR Team member, a twelve hour or twenty-four hour period on duty. A shift for a firefighter is based on the "A-B-C" schedule. Firefighters work a twenty-four hour shift and then have forty-eight hours off.

Station – The station is where CR Team members, firefighters, and command and support personnel are based for the duration of their shifts. It can contain four to eight firefighters, two rescue-unit members, sometimes a battalion chief and captain, and two CR Team members. The typical station has a kitchen, private sleeping rooms (in the newer facilities), a lounge/entertainment area, a large dining area, and a workout room. Some stations even have racquetball courts, large office and administrative areas, and community rooms.

Warm Fuzzies – A sensation of sharing a moment of good feeling, kindness, and caring with each other.

Acknowledgments

This book, as with most books, has many people behind the scenes.

To my parents, who raised me to the best of their abilities.... I was more than a handful, but your love was always there for me, guiding me to do what was right. In our small pond of life, you gave me an ocean of love. You are the light that leads the way for me and the many others with whom you come in contact daily.

To my husband, Yale, who has supported me through all of this.... Your love, patience, and wonderful mind have shown me that I can have it all in life as long as you are by my side. You complete me. Who would have thought that a psychic-trauma junkie and a laid-back nuclear engineer could hook up and make life and love work so well together?

To my son, Michael, his wife, Danielle, and my grandboys, Bradley and Calvin.... I know I'm a bit "weird," but perhaps "eccentric" would be a better description from now on!

To my daughter, Rebecca, her husband, Dustin, and my grandaughter, Madysen Emalee.... Abilities run strong in the family female line, so I wish you all the best throughout the years ahead.

To my brothers, Robert and Jaime.... Childhood was too short, but the momeries will last forever. Thank you for the deep, bonding sense of strength and family we share with each other.

To Anna May Cottrell.... For your inspiration and teachings. You are the best psychic, medium and intuitive I have ever met. Your classes opened my mind and my soul. My parents showed me the world. You introduced me to the universe and beyond.

To Stacy Laabs....Who kept me focused through her endless and caring phone calls to keep forging ahead with this unusual undertaking, and for assisting me in the evolution of its title. You rock, Girl!

Thank you all. *Namaste!*

Also from New River Press

Turning Home

God, Ghosts and Human Destiny

By Paul F. Eno

Ultimate questions - Ultimate answers!
Who are you? Where will you go when you die? Where are your loved ones who already have? Who is God? Why are we the way we are? Why is God the way God is? *Is* there a God? In this astounding, information-packed book, an award-winning journalist, seminary graduate and 35-year paranormal investigator offers answers that could transform your life, and maybe the whole world.

"A coalescence of Paul F. Eno's decades of study of the paranormal, theology, psychology and philosophy, Turning Home *provides the keys to understanding life, death and reality – and to living in a way that will enhance the multiverse in which we all exist. This book will convince you beyond a doubt that there is more to life than the archetype to which most of us subscribe!*
-Antoinette Kuritz
Host, Writers Roundtable, World Talk Radio

ISBN 1-891724-06-1
ISBN-13 978-1-891724-06-0

www.turninghome.net

$16.95 suggested retail price
Buy online or through your favorite bookstore

Also from New River Press,
those two classics of the paranormal:

Faces at the Window

First-Hand Accounts of the Paranormal in
Southern New England

and

Footsteps in the Attic

More First-Hand Accounts of the Paranormal
in New England

Paul F. Eno

By an award-winning journalist who has spent over 35 years stalking the paranormal, these are two of the most unusual books ever written about ghosts.
Follow Eno (author of *Turning Home: God, Ghosts and Human Destiny*) through 22 cases he personally investigated,
and see his mind-expanding interpretation of what they mean. Eno terrifies the soul, dazzles the mind and touches the heart.

www.footstepsintheattic.com

FACES: Suggested Retail Price: $12.95
ISBN: 1-891724-01-0, ISBN 13: 978-1-891724-01-5
FOOTSTEPS: Suggested Retail Price: $14.95
ISBN: 1-891724-02-9, ISBN 13: 978-1-891724-02-2

Buy online or through your favorite bookstore

Also from New River Press

41 SIGNS of Hope

By Dave Kane

From New England talk-show host Dave Kane, father of Nick O'Neill, youngest of the 100 victims of the disastrous 2003 Station nightclub fire in Rhode Island, comes a book full of hope that our loved ones do not die. After the passing of this gifted young man came a series of amazing "coincidences" based on the number 41, his favorite number. Through a long series of startling incidents and heart-warming happenings, Nick has proven his presence and the eternal nature of family love!
A must-read for anyone who has
lost a loved one!
www.41signsofhope.com
Suggested Retail Price: $14.95
ISBN: 1-891724-05-3
ISBN 13: 978-1-891724-05-3
Buy online or through your favorite bookstore

Coming from New River Press
for the Holiday Season, 2006

Letters from Legends

and the
Incredible Interviews
that Inspired Them

by award-winning celebrity journalist

Marian Christy

These previously unpublished letters to the author by major figures in government, show business and the media, based on her eye-opening interviews with them, will keep you glued to this amazing book from beginning to end. Included are Richard Nixon, Jerry Lewis, Tom Brokaw, Yoko Ono, Corretta Scott King, Dan Rather, Joan Crawford, Jacqueline Kennedy Onassis, and many, many more!

www.lettersfromlegends.com
Suggested Retail Price: $18.95
ISBN: 1-891724-07-X
ISBN 13: 978-1-891724-07-7
Buy online or through your favorite bookstore